YOUR FUTURE, IS YOU

Your Potential, Makes You

Pleasing Your Life Cause, Assignment, and Ambition

YOUR FUTURE IS YOU
(Your Potential, Makes You)

Copyright © 20......................

ISBN: ....

Published by: Dominion Publishers

Email:

. . . .

. . . .

DEDICATION

AKNOWLEDGEMENT

All glory and honour is worthy to the **Most High God** for the inspiration, the source of every good and perfect gift he has given to me.

All the praise and glory towards making this book a reality also goes to my Lord and Saviour **Jesus Christ** for choosing me to serve Him in spite of my flaws and frailties and the **Holy Spirit** for His divine guidance and counsel.

I am of the opinion that credits to every inspired piece must be jointly shared, as it is always a product of concerted efforts, my **beloved** ...... and **confidant,** .... and *family,* you are God's gift to me and the pillar of my strength and the shoulder I always cry on in my walk with God and Maker.

I sincerely want to appreciate my Dear Father and Mentor, *Pastor Joseph U. White*, the Chief Executive officer of **Potter's Place (South Africa)** who worked tirelessly with me to see to the success of this noble work, he is a genius and an enigma of creative ideas.

My profound appreciation to all my *friends, Colleagues and partners* in the work of God all over the world.

PREFACE

In order to get to the heart of who you truly are, you need to be able to imagine your true potential and discover who you really are. You need to develop and then implement a plan of action. You need to create your own mastermind team and find coaches and mentors to help you through the muddy waters of life. You need to create affirmations that support your life's purpose. You need to be able to envision your desired outcome and learn how to feel gratitude once again.

When you learn how to tap into the Universal Law of Attraction, as it pertains to your unique goals and visions, you can create a roadmap to your success, a map that you can easily follow. Fulfilling your life's purpose is all about tapping into the flow of energy all around you. It's about finding a frame of reference that you can use as a lifelong learning system.

Finding your life purpose is all about tapping into your spiritual identity. It's about realizing your true potential. It's about finding solutions that help you navigate difficult waters. It's about making a difference and leaving a legacy. It's much more than just positive thinking and daydreaming. It's really about empowerment. It's about finding and living your truth. It's about reaching deep inside yourself and rediscovering who you are. It's about harnessing your creative power and coming from a place of love, rather than pain.

Are you steadily working towards your destiny and fulfilling your life purpose or have you gotten lost along the way? Has life challenged you to the point that you have lost your sense of enthusiasm and passion? Are you tired of drifting aimlessly through your days? Do you want a better life, but just don't know how to get there; do you want to be *Essential* and *Relevant* to your generation, community and society? Then this book in your hand is just the answer to your questions.

If you are not living your best life or attaining your potentials in life, you can change the course of your life easily and effortlessly, the only thing that can make you essential, is your potential because you are ultimately in control of your future. You are 100% responsible for your life, no matter what. If you have a desire to change the course of your life, and you want to fulfil your life's purpose and rediscover your life's task and goals, you need to take back control of your life by banking on your potentials.

In order to rediscover your life's purpose, you have to figure out and discover what your passions are, what your dreams are. It is easy to get off track, because life is very complex. Everyone has unique talents and gifts but we sometimes forget what those are along the way. Some people are born knowing their unique Potentials/talents while others have to dig a little deeper to discover theirs.

Discovering your life Potential/Purpose is like going on an amazing journey, a treasure hunt. It's about being authentic to who you really are, at the deepest level of your core. It's about finding your personal vision and rediscovering your passions. It's about setting S.M.A.R.T. goals that provide you with a map that you can actually follow. Finding your life potential/purpose can literally transform your life & make you essential & relevant to your generation. It can help you get excited about your life once again. Once you figure out what your unique gifts and passions are, you will be on fire for life.

The need to eradicate ignorance from the lives of people is also one major reason to the writing of the book in your hand. It has been discovered that a lot of people die due to ignorance concerning the purpose and the special potentials/gifts of God in their lives. The few ones that are still alive are still held spell bound by this same ignorance.

A lot of people, who still depend on the economy of the nation today to meet their ends, would have been on top; if they had received the right information. As it is known that lack of information leads to deformation; while information leads to reformation and promotion. Today, we see more of Methuselah's around us living a good number of years on the surface of the earth with just one line of record than

David who discovered himself at the early stage of his life and made a lot of records in the bible. It is imperative to say that people suffer more from lack of purpose than lack of money. It pains me so much each time I remember the particular word of preacher, **thus***; the grave yard is the richest place on earth because many unfulfilled potentials, talents, destiny, visions are buried there.* Great books that would have been written, talents/potentials that worth's Billions of **Rands or Dollars** are buried everyday in the graveyard. It is my privilege to inform you that the book in your hand will give you the key to discover your naturally endowed **Potential/Talent** that will make you Relevant & **Essential in life.**

More so, this book contains the phases of every destiny that must be fulfilled and the steps to follow. Utilize each of them perfectly. Perhaps, you are still in search of your Potential/Talent, and are still confused about your destiny; do not hesitate to read this book, as solutions are fully loaded in it.

Perhaps, you have lost hope about your talent and the realization of your dreams in life, are you still confused about your destiny; do not hesitate to read this book, as solutions are fully loaded in it.

Perhaps, you have lost hope about your potential/talent and the realization of your dream to stand out in life, there is still hope of recovery.

 "A man's belly shall be satisfied with the fruit of his mouth; and with the increase of his lips, shall he be filled. Death and life is in the power of the tongue; and they that love it shall eat the fruit thereof." Proverbs 18:20-21

Permit me to emphasis at this point that it is the reader's right to judge whether or not the conclusions which I have drawn in the forthcoming pages are justified. Some may disagree, and disagree strongly, with my reasoning's, but this book must have served its purpose by inspiring honest opinion on every important subject therein, it is my sincere desire that all readers of this book will be encouraged to learn and obey God from the pages of history as relative to this book.

Treasured Friend, the freedom brought to humanity by a single decision taken by our Lord and Savour Jesus Christ cannot be over emphasized, therefore I will enjoin you to open up your heart as you explore the pages of this book, I am very sure the Holy Spirit will grant you insight into every mystery deposited in this book,

Be Sanctified!

Chapter One

Knowing What You Have

Potential comes from the root words *"potency"* and *"potent"* and refers to all the things you can be successful at if you develop and use your *gifts, talents and natural abilities.*

The word *"potential"* can have several meanings. That said, the meaning you are talking about, is related to how much a person could achieve or accomplish, given the *proper motivation, resources and opportunities.*

I believe we all have untapped potential within us. Though we try every day to be the best we can be, the habits of daily life get in the way of realizing our true potential that will eventually make us relevant & essential in our community and society. You may be wondering in what ways can you exploit your potential and clear the distractions from your life, so as to allow your potential make you relevant and essential to your community and generation.

Some people have only a small potential, because of intellectual or physical problems and challenges or difficulties/deficiencies. Other people who are for example, very intelligent, or who have genes which permit them to run quickly or gain muscle mass very easily, or who have extra-ordinary abilities in the area of language or mathematics or music, have very large or great potential: given the right motivation, will, opportunities and access to resources, they can achieve wonderful or at least above average things!!

Jesus did not teach man how to make a living but taught man how to live. God doesn't call us to be successful; He calls us to be faithful. God do not see us as failures but as learners. God has three meals; His breakfast: our obedience towards His words (in secret and in open) or worshiping Him in Spirit and in Truth (John 4:24) His lunch: appreciation, thanksgiving and praises unto Him. His dinner: – paying our tithes, offerings and investing into the lives of others.

On the last day, God will ask us three main questions

- What did you do with His son Jesus Christ while you were here on   earth?

- What did you do with your potentials and talents?

- What did you do with your fellow men while you were living?

Know that your godliness in the secret is the main key of your relationship with your God than your open godliness. God dwells more in the secret than open. Live with a clean hand and a pure heart and you will be closer unto God Almighty. ***"If you draw closer to Him, He will draw closer unto you" James 4:8***

The main factors to be considered when describing any person on the surface of this earth are as follows: *Attitude, Belief, and Environment.* For a person to move from inferior level to superior level or mediocre to excellence, he or she must surely possess these values: Desire, enthusiasm, and persistence in his or her entire existence. If a man wants to attain marvellous accomplishments in life, he or she needs to possess these values: self-discipline, sacrifice and a fighting spirit in his or her life.

Truly speaking numerous shocking things have gone wrong in life whereby fear, ignorance, greed, procrastination, distraction, purposelessness, doubt, directionless, discouragements, hopelessness lack of these: self-confidence, vision, knowledge and prompt action have consummately engulfed man's existence because they are far from their creator – the Almighty God. These are lack of positive mental attitude and good values in life.

When a man can't control his mind positively and wisely utilize his or her time in life, he or she has missed the correct pathway to successful living. The strong room of man's existence is the mind (heart); that is why negative influence, fear, and self-destructive behaviours are quick tools to human destruction in life.

God have given mankind three greatest gift. Grace (coming of the Lord Jesus Christ to save and redeem mankind) mind and time! Before now all philosophers believe that God's gifts are two: mind and time.

One of the greatest things that can happen unto mankind is self-actualization (self-realization). Next, keep right and then believe, be bold, be smart, make use of your inner eyes (third eye), pursue your goals with your mental strength or brain power not physical strength or body power in life. Make use of your sixth sense – which is common sense

that is called abundance of wisdom cleverly make good use of your small still voice or silence voice it truly pays in greater measure in life.

Always look inward to beautify your outward existence. This level of being in-the inner state produces the outer condition. Good breeds good, bad produces bad. In life, the power of cause and effects-comes to play. Whereby the cause is the thoughts while the effect is the condition in consequences of those thoughts that a man exercises in life.

Always make sure you know the sources and kinds of information you permit into your mind which is the engine room of a living soul because that singular act will determine whether you are building positive attitude or negative attitude. Right information produces positive mental attitude if applied accordingly while wrong information produces negative mental attitude when wrongly applied in life. Life is basically centred on your choice and decisions you always make in your life (existence). Always make sure you are making right choices or decisions because it explains your life to the world in general.

Tremendous act of men that have been wrong and destructive are based on them not knowing themselves, others and even the environment they live in. Napoleon Hill said: the greatest failure of men is the act of men exposing their minds to the negative influence of others. He went further again and said that: the failure of men doesn't consist on the money or possession he doesn't have but failure to know who he or she is in life.

Napoleon Hill likens the situation of men as: man got himself locked in prison and remove the key and place it inside his pocket and started to look out who will set him free from the prison.

People basically live by sight instead of living by faith (II Corinthians 5:7). They live in the world without instead of them to live in the world within. They pursue shadows instead of reality of life. They believe in luck instead of believing in causes and effects. They don't know that every source of great attainment, accomplishment and achievement mainly dwell inside of them than they constantly pursue their success outside. The greatest embracing strategies in life are as follows: embrace life time learning, embrace thinking positively and acting promptly and embracing change and taking risk.

The beginning of knowing what you have is to centre on first, the ability to control one's mind positively. Secondly, the ability to manage one's time judiciously and willingness to preserve one's body to the glory of God in life. Most men are only interested in the blessings and gifts of God not in Him (God), the giver of those marvellous favour and blessing in life.

They are good at counting their problems instead of counting their blessings in life.

For you to function properly with what you have, you need to observe these three greatest duties of mankind: unto God be faithful, unto yourself be sincere and unto others be truthful.

What you have is greatly classified into three aspects: who you are (purpose or mission in life), what you are (potentials and talents) and where you are (available opportunities inside out). If one smartly takes the advantages of them, it will lead one to a greater height of success, prosperity, happiness and healthiness in life. Personal greatness is gotten by discovering one's potentials and using them to influence the lives of others positively. The ability to utilize these areas of life that is what you have (potentials, purpose and opportunities) will expressly produce pathway to one's success and accomplishment in life. You need to build your life upon these great values that will help you to build and keep your life: Love, patience and courage. Know it clearly that love and patience are the parents of virtues in life. Only build upon love then other virtues will move up to the level of its existence because the level of love produces the level of other existing virtues of life. Shut up your love, patience, courage, self-control, right choice, right decision, constructive desire and thoughts even rest of the notable virtues in life will move to the same equilibrium. Know it clearly that positive mental attitude is everything in life. You need to build it into your life by knowing the features and attributes of positive mental attitude that will be treated in the coming chapter.

The motto of nature: is keep on moving or you perish. The motto of life: a winner never quits and quitters never win. The motto of existence: be a master of your fate and captain of your soul. Your decisions determine your destiny, your habits determine your future, while your choices determines your existence in life.

Note this great word said by John Mason "only hungry minds grow" he further said "the bigger your obstacles, the better your opportunity in life". No obstacle will keep you the way it met you, it either takes you up or down, but your attitude towards it will determine your success or failure in life (John Mason)

The facts that face us are not important but the attitude we put towards them determines our success or failure in life (Normal Vincent Pearl) our success, prosperity and happiness greatly depend on our fighting spirit. The biggest question is not what have happened to us but what we do to what have happened to us

(George Allan). James Allan said "the mind of a man is like a soil; whatsoever you plant inside must surely grow, but if you refuse to plant anything weeds must grow thereby, so you need to constantly keep on weeding those weeds (negative mental attitude, negative behaviour, destructive desire and thoughts, wrong choice and decisions etc.)

How to Build What You Have

The facts remain that the information you possess truly builds your mind, and that produces the kind of character, habits, motives, beliefs, desire, self-talk, self-esteem, decision and choice you manifest in your entire existence. Mind and time have been considered by great philosophers as what God have used to bless mankind but recent research and revelations carried out by myself came out with the third gift that became the first before mind and time, which is Grace.

(The coming of the Lord Jesus Christ); that have bestowed mercy, love and the graciousness of the almighty God unto human beings all over the world. The virtues that man possesses are numerous to count; they are infinite or unlimited in number. These virtues exist inside or outside of a man. So until a man consciously search from the inside (man's mind) he or she will remain poor and experience great lack those beautiful and attractive virtues that dwell much inside of his or her mind. Man need to reach out to what is inside(infinite intelligent or invisible realm or inner world or the subconscious mind of man's existence) listen to his or her still small voice, use his or her third eye, and utilize his/ her sixth sense which is called common sense, that is abundance of wisdom. Men have failed in life, because they are far from their creator which has resulted to *great distraction, ignorance, fear and procrastination* in their existence. This situation has brought about them chasing after physical or material things (seen issues) than spiritual or heavenly things (un-seen issues). They basically pursue shadows leaving the realities of life. They strongly believe in what they can possibly see and touch not believing what they can feel with their mind that expresses greater and marvellous things of human existence. They chase after money leaving developing ideas or dreams that they can turn into action or existence to fetch a unique result in life.

Helen Keller said: *The best and beautiful things are not what we touch or see with our hands, but what a man truly feels with his mind.* She also said that: *Life is a daring adventure or nothing. They believe in scarcity and not in abundance;* where they supposed to launch themselves into the subconscious mind or infinite intelligence where all great virtues dwell richly.

In life what you have consist of: who you are-purpose, what you are-potential, and where you are-your opportunities in life. The moment you understand these basic facts of human existence and tap into its chamber, you have won over untold struggles, pains and worries of life. You need to know about human needs, human challenges and human attributes, they are very vital to a successful existence of any person.

Whether your circumstances are favourable or unfavourable, you only need to confront them with positive mental attitude and good values, you will surely attain success at the end of the confrontation. A man said: 90% of the woes this world has are as a result of people living all the days of their existence without knowing themselves or what they really have in life.

James William said that: he has discovered the greatest thing in life that a man can alter his life by altering the attitude of his mind. Napoleon Hill said: whatsoever a man's mind covets and believe must be achieved in life. Frank Tiger said: your future depends on so many things especially on you.

Dr Frank Crena said: *your best friends and your worst enemies are thoughts you have about yourself.*

When a man would possess personal developing strategies is whereby he spends enough time to study great books like the Bible, motivational books and professional books; and then apply the laws, principles and strategies written thereby. He or she will surely experience growth, self-improvement and great development in his or her entire existence.

Our Lord Jesus Christ said to all, that all things are possible to him that believeth (mark 9:23). You can't really know your purpose, identify your talents and recognize limitless opportunities and needs without you knowing your creator the almighty God. And for one to pay the price; that is exercising these unique virtues: *self-discipline, desire, sacrifice, enthusiasm, optimism, commitment, determination, dedication, faithfulness, integrity, maturity, intelligence, direction, focus, conviction, courtesy, patience, courage, persistence, kindness, sincerity and truthfulness, hard work, working smartly, vision, diligent, love and prompt action.*

You can't just attain this level of human existence without self-discipline, sacrifice, courage, patience, purpose and a fighting spirit! That is coupled with God's favour. The strength of recognition, appreciation, vision, knowledge and application must come to play in one's life to actualize the level of self-realization in existence.

CHAPTER TWO

Giving Birth to a Vision

We can exploit our potential when we allow our natural gifting and tendency to develop and mature. God has placed in each one of us unique gifts and talents and we find our highest place of usefulness when we use these gifts for His glory. We should not try to imitate somebody else who may have a different gifting from ours.

Having then gifts differing according to the grace that is given to us, whether prophecy, let us prophesy according to the proportion of faith; Or ministry, let us wait on our ministering: or he that teacheth, on teaching; Or he that exhorteth, on exhortation: he that giveth, let him do it with simplicity; he that ruleth, with diligence; he that sheweth mercy, with cheerfulness. Romans 12:6-8 (KJV)

We can make best use of our potential when we get our encouragement from God. Peter preached to the Gentiles under the direction of God even though many other apostles misunderstood him. We should not allow the fear of man to prevent us from obeying God and fulfilling His destiny in our lives.

"And the Spirit bade me go with them, nothing doubting. Moreover these six brethren accompanied me, and we

entered into the man's house:" Acts 11:12 (KJV)

"Forasmuch then as God gave them the like gift as he did unto us, who believed on the Lord Jesus Christ; what was I, that I could withstand God?" Acts 11:17 (KJV)

We can capitalize on our potential when allow only positive influence in our life. The apostles had unusual boldness through their association with Jesus. We should avoid coming under the influence of negative people such as *murmurers, critics, doubters, fearful, rebellious etc.* Negative people have never achieved anything in their life. They only find fault and are envious of those who have achieved something. If we want to maximize our potential when must be careful to be under positive influence.

"Blessed is the man that walketh not in the counsel of the ungodly, nor standeth in the way of sinners, nor sitteth in the seat of the scornful. But his delight is in the law of the LORD; and in his law doth he meditate day and night. And he shall be like a tree planted by the rivers of water, that bringeth forth his fruit in his season; his leaf also shall not wither; and whatsoever he doeth shall prosper".
Psalms 1:1-3 (KJV)

We can exploit our potential when we are inventive. The friends of the paralytic man found an innovative way to reach Jesus by opening the roof. We should not give up when the natural ways and doors are closed. We should become innovative and find new ways of doing things and increasing our usefulness.

"And they come unto him, bringing one sick of the palsy, which was borne of four. 4 And when they could not come

nigh unto him for the press, they uncovered the roof where he was: and when they had broken it up, they let down the bed wherein the sick of the palsy lay. 5 When Jesus saw their faith, he said unto the sick of the palsy, Son, thy sins be forgiven thee". Mark 2:3-5 (KJV)

We can take full advantage of our potential when we take the initiative and not wait for someone to push us. Jesus took the initiative to go through the cities and villages preaching the gospel. He did not wait for somebody to encourage Him or push Him forward. We can maximize our potential if we are willing to take the initiative to make ourselves useful to the kingdom of God.

"He that observeth the wind shall not sow; and he that regardeth the clouds shall not reap. As thou knowest not what is the way of the spirit, nor how the bones do grow in the womb of her that is with

child: even so thou knowest not the works of God who maketh all. In the morning sow thy seed, and in the evening withhold not thine hand: for thou knowest not whether shall prosper, either this or that, or whether they both shall be alike good". Eccl 11:4-7 (KJV)

We can take full advantage of our potential when we receive instruction in areas where we are ignorant. There may be many areas where we are ignorant and we should not hesitate to receive counsel from competent people who have experience and expertise in those areas where we are ignorant. Otherwise we will waste time and resources struggling in areas where we are ignorant. We can maximize our potential by receiving timely instruction.

14 Where no counsel is, the people fall: but in the multitude of counsellors there is safety. Prov 11:14 (KJV)

We can make best use of our potential when our efforts are undergirded by prayer. A farmer ploughs the field but he still needs the rain to get his harvest. In the same way all our labours will go in vain if we do not receive the showers of God's blessing through our fervent prayers. *"The effectual fervent prayer of a righteous man availeth much."* We can maximize our potential by undergirding our efforts with prayers and intercessions.

"So admit your sins to each other, and pray for each other so that you will be healed. Prayers offered by those who have God's approval are effective. Elijah was human like us. Yet, when he prayed that it wouldn't rain, no rain fell on the ground for three-and-a-half years. Then he prayed again. It rained, and the

ground produced crops". James 5:16-18 (GW)

Having established the relevance of knowing what you have, we shall be considering how to acquire a personal vision. These are the necessary steps towards becoming who God created you to be. It is the step every great man has taken in life and it is the step you must also take if you must not die empty.

Prayers

"Commit thy ways unto the Lord" psalms 37 v 5

God is the source of all good vision and dreams. He alone holds your life and future in His Mighty hands. He created you with your unique strength and attributes and He knows your end from the day you were conceived in your mother's womb. Therefore, the number one step towards acquiring a vision is to go to Him in prayers to seek His face.

King Solomon (1kings 3 v 5-9) made a very wise decision when he became king in Israel. The Bible says God appeared to him in a dream and all he asked for was wisdom, direction and help in the governance of His people. What he got from that experience was vision. The success and prosperity of Solomon's reign was not unconnected to this step. When you bow your knees to God in prayers to seek a vision for your life, what you are simply doing is inviting the light from above to meet the light from below in your inner man. He causes your inner man to receive insight and inspiration that would otherwise elude you. Job 32 v 8: says that "but there is a spirit in man and the breadth of the almighty gives understanding".

Jesus Christ our Saviour and Lord spent forty days and forty nights in the wilderness seeking God's face for His ministry on earth (Mathew 4) when it was time for His disciples to be chosen, He also withdrew to a mountain to pray (Luke 6: 12-16) every disciple was chosen on purpose to fulfil pre-determined task. Judas for example was chosen on purpose to betray the master. All these were gotten on the altar of withdrawal and separation unto to God.

Lastly, Apostle Paul's ministry was birthed in the desert of Arabia (Galatians 1 v 17) where he went and spent three years. The blueprint and master plan of his vision was presented to him right there in the desert. He knew the extent of his suffering for the Gospel and of his ministry before he undertook his first missionary journey. Great visions are not birthed in palaces or in the comfort of plenty; rather they are brought to pass in the deep recess of man's soul to his maker.

So, right always get on your knees and ask your creator to open your eyes to His plan and purpose for your life.

Sometimes you may not know exactly what to pray about, this is the time to lock out your senses and begin to pray in the Holy Ghost. Inspiration flourishes in the place of speaking in other tongues; your spirit man is praying and making contact with divinity. You assess and unlock real treasures hitherto hidden from you in the place of praying in tongues

"Great Visions Are Not Birthed In Palaces or In The Comfort Of Plenty".

The Word

"Search the scriptures for in them ye think ye have life." John 5 : 39

The bible has been rightly described as life's manual and also as the manufacturer's handbook for living. It is God's instruction for man and the wise man will take its contents very seriously. No other person should be addicted to studying God's Word like a man who desires a vision for his life. In the book of Hebrews chapter 10 v 7, it say's "according to what has been written concerning me in the volume of books; I have to come to do thy will o Lord" There are certain things written concerning you that you can only have access to by studying the scriptures. It is by studying God's Word that you understand what your maker has created you to be and to have. As you go through the Bible, you will discover some truths about yourself that no other person will ever tell you. Daniel for instance understood by "Books" that the children of Israel were to spend only seventy years in captivity of Babylon. This prompted his seeking God's face for the deliverance of his people. In Daniel 9 v 2, the Bible say's ***"in the first year of his reign, I Daniel*** *understood by books the number of the years whereby the Word of the Lord came to Jeremiah the prophet, that he would accomplish seventy years in the desolation of Jerusalem"* par-adventure the children of Israel would have stayed longer than necessary in Babylon if Daniel had not studied the scroll to know their time of deliverance. It is time for you also to leave captivity by understanding from God's Word that you have been liberated from sickness, pain and poverty.

The children of Issachar were more noble than their brethren because they had understanding of times and seasons (1 chronicle 12 v 32) because of this, they had their brethren at their commands. The time table of your life is in the Word of God; your life's schedule has been revealed in the Holy Bible: go search it out, you can no longer allow the deceiver-Satan the devil to lock you up in the prison of ignorance, you have been declared the head and not the tail, to be above only and not beneath. You have been declared rich because through Christ's poverty though He was rich, you became wealthy. Dust off the shame of backwardness and become all God has made you to be. It is all in the Word.

There was a story of a man on-board on a ship, he paid the required fare and boarded the ship. He saw other passengers ordering for their meals but he contented himself with the meagre meal he had managed to bring along. This went on for days until one of the passengers noticed him and tried to find out why he was not ordering his meal from the attendants in the ship. He answered very quietly that he could not afford the meals being served. He did not know that when he paid for the ticket for the ship, his meals were already paid for too. What ignorance!

"Your Vision Is In the Word Locate It"

Meditation

"For as he thinketh in his heart, so is he". Proverbs 23 : 7

Meditation is defined as the practice of thinking deeply in silence. It means to ponder on, ruminate on and to fix your mind on something. It is a characteristic of the spiritual mind. Meditation helps to open doors to the unseen word and makes it real to our physical sense. The scriptures say that "as a man thinketh in his heart, so is he" you cannot think like an ant and live like an elephant. You cannot think like a victim and ever hope to be a victor, everything you will become in life starts from your mind. If you cannot accommodate something big in your imagination, you cannot obtain it. It is a simple law of nature. The battle of life is fought in the mind. You win first in your mind before you can become a conqueror in real life. Little wonder then that the enemy attacks your mind by telling you lies about what you cannot do and what you cannot become in life. The moment you agree with him in your mind, he has succeeded in robbing you of your destiny.

Your meditation will make or mar you. The reason is simple: your mind is like a garden and it grows whatever is planted on it whether good or bad. You must therefore seek to plant good thoughts on the soil of your mind for you to reap good things. Out of the twelve spies sent to Canaan, ten of them saw themselves as grasshoppers before the children of Anak and so they were (numbers 13 v 33). They lost the battle in their minds, caused the entire nation of Israel to grieve bitterly. Joshua and Caleb on the other hand saw the battle differently and considered the battle for Canaan won in their minds. Sit quietly away from hustling and bustling of the modern world and think deeply about your life. Think about your tomorrow, your dream job and home. What can you see in the realm of your thoughts? Can't you see that you are a success waiting to manifest, a solution to a problem and an answer to a need? Have you ever thought about your unique strength and attributes and how they are able to lift you up to your place in life? Think my brother, think my sister; the world is anxiously waiting for you. As you engage your mental faculty in the business of mediation, three things must occupy your mind.

The Lord: He is the centre of our lives. When you meditate on Him, He opens your eyes of understanding to see things that are not open to the natural eyes.

The Word: Reading and studying the scripture is not enough, God told Joshua (Joshua 1:8) that to be prosperous in one's way requires meditation on His Word.

God's Work: Jesus told us that greater works than He did we would do. So, as you meditate on the works of God, you begin to see how you can accomplish your work here on planet earth.

Association:

"And being let go, they went to their own company…" Acts 4 v 23"

The influence of association on a man cannot be overemphasized. All over the world, people are talking about networking and alignment for mutual benefit. Large companies are merging for greater effectiveness, countries are forming alliances and individuals are coming together to harness their resources. This is a way of achieving seemingly difficult and impossible tasks. One of the main benefits of right association is in the area of vision acquisition, your association will go a long way to either improve your lot in life or otherwise. You cannot afford to be surrounded by people who will kill your dreams and consider what you hold dear as nothing. From such people, flea. Right association is that which will fire your aspirations and encourage you towards your dreams.

People have drawn aspirations from simply associating with the right people; some have had their destinies put back on course by the people God brought their way. Many individuals have climbed the ladder of success by simply stepping on the shoulders of others who have gone before them. You can drink from the fountain of wisdom of elders and thereby acquire your own dreams and vision. In acts of the apostles, Aquila and Pricilla took a young and zealous minister into their house and taught him so many things and guarded him on the right path to follow (Acts 18 v 26) says "whom when

Aquila and Pricilla had heard, they took him unto them and expounded unto him the way of the Lord more perfectly". This is an example of the power of right association.

The place of this couple in the life of this young man can never be forgotten. As a young man or woman seeking a vision, you need to associate with a mentor. Your mentor should be more experienced than you in matters of life, should have your respect and obedience. This is the bone of most youths these days. No one wants to be under the influence of others. It is a wrong way to follow if you must be a successful person.

I know a young man who today is a success in the legal profession. However, in his early years in the secondary school, he associated with the wrong set of persons and was subsequently corrupted. He joined a secret cult and was drifting fast away from his destiny. However, he met the Lord Jesus and began to re-associate with people of great minds and today he is an embodiment of legal success.

The scripture further says "He that walketh with the wise shall be wise; but a company of fools shall be destroyed" (Proverbs 13 v 20). If you associate with the wrong people, destruction awaits you; but if you associate with great, visionary and Godly persons, you will become great "The Company of fools shall be destroyed".

5 DREAMS: A dream is a sequence of mental images during sleep; it could involve activities in one's past or future events. A dream most times is as real as the physical world. It has profound effect on us and affects our entire being.

Many of the Old Testament prophets received revelation and divine messages through dreams, a lot of times God speaks to man through dreams. Joseph is a perfect example of birthing a vision with dreams. At seventeen years of age, he had two different dreams each depicting in very vivid forms his future.

He clung to these dreams tenaciously and each experience he had in life was put in proper perspective; because he had seen his future and what he would be in his dreams. In Mathew chapter 2 v 13, Joseph the husband of Mary received warning from God to take baby Jesus to Egypt for security reasons. When it was time to return to Israel, it was through dreams. As a man seeking a vision for life, one of the strong avenues to receive one is through dreams.

You can see yourself or your tomorrow in your dreams; you can peep into God's plan for your life through dreams. Positive dreams are part of the tools of a man with vision. Do not neglect your dreams for they say a lot about your future. However, every dream should be cross checked with God's Word. Discard any dream if it is not in consonance with His Word.

6 YOUR PASSION: Passion is defined as a strong liking or enthusiasm for a subject or activity. It is that element that drives you to do the things you do and it also defines how you do them. It is a strong pointer to what you are created to do and become in life. Different people have different passions and it under-scores the different visions we all have. What you are drawn or attracted to gives a clear indication of your vision. If you keep doing what you like and enjoy, you will soon discover your area of calling. There is a woman I know who is easily touched by the pain and suffering of others. She will go out of her way to alleviate the suffering of others even if it means

sacrificing her comfort. She does this with so much joy and fulfilment. No wonder she has a vision of building orphanages and old people's home. This is just an example of how your passion can open your eyes to birthing a personal vision. "Your passion is a strong pointer to what you are created to do and become in life".

7 SEEING A NEED: The ability to see and locate a need is very important in acquiring a vision. Needs abound and will always remain with man as long as we are on this side of eternity. The economist say that man's needs are insatiable and resources are scarce. It is a very true statement because as one need is being met, another is discovered. Many of man's inventions come as answers to man's needs. The need to travel from one place to the other gave birth to the different means of transportation. The need to overcome darkness let to the discovery of

electricity and the list goes on and on. Moses took a stroll one sunny afternoon in Egypt. As he walked by, he saw an Egyptian maltreating an Israelite; he quickly came to the Israelites rescue and killed the Egyptian. He saw a need and though responded wrongly but it propelled his vision for the deliverance of the children of Israel from the bondage of Egypt. David in 1 Samuel 17 v 17-27 was sent to see how his brothers were faring at the battle front. When he got there, he heard goliath insulting the army of the children of Israel. He asked people standing by what would be given to the man who will kill goliath. He also saw a need and responded accordingly. That formed his vision of eliminating the enemy of God's people.

If you can see a need and you have a strong desire to meet that need, you are on the verge of creating a vision for yourself.

Vision built on solving a need will always remain entrenched in the hearts of men for generations to come. Inventors we all remember today were those that solved a need or the other through their works. As you go about today and always, open your senses to the needs all around you and develop a desire to meet these needs. You can as well be the next great inventor the world is waiting for.

"Any vision built on solving a need will always remain entrenched in the hearts of men for generations to come".

Chapter Three

How to Achieve Your Vision

The A – Z Of Vision

A: ATTEMPT YOUR VISION

"Whatsoever thy hand findeth to do, do it with all your might" Eccl 9 v 10

Once you have found a vision, apply your hands to see it come to pass. No matter how big your vision is, until it is attempted it is of no good at all. Do not do the talk, do the vision! Some people specialize in telling others about their tall dreams without putting their hands to work. Such dreams will never come to reality. A vision not attempted dies in the heart of the visionary. You may never know what that vision is capable of turning into. The major difference between a dreamer and a goal-getter is that the latter goes to work with his vision while the former just talk about his. Don't end up just being a dreamer! Turn that dream into a tangible reality by doing something about it now. Vision without a corresponding action will breed frustration.

You may not know in details what your vision entails: you may not have all the resources to execute that tall ambition of yours at the moment, but begin from where you are and what you have now. There is always a starting point for every vision. Do not neglect your days of little beginning for if you stick to it, it shall grow. Remember as they say; Rome was not built in a day. Do you have a multi-million-dollar project and all you have right now is a few cents? Don't despair; remember that the widow of Zarephath had only a few cup of flour and little bottle of oil. She later became a flour dealer and an oil magnate! All she did was to start with that few cups of flour and the little bottle of oil with the prophets blessing and the result was mind blowing. Every big thing in life started small. The human body for instance started as an embryo that continued to divide and grow into the different cells of the body. The human race started with a couple Adam and Eve in the Garden of Eden. The list is endless "Every big thing in life started small".

B: BELIEVE IN YOUR VISION

"Jesus said unto him, if you can believe all things are possible to him that believes" mark 9 v 23.

The only way you can actualize your vision is to believe in it. There is no vision that cannot be brought into fruition if one believes in the vision and in God. Believe in the peculiarity and the possibility of your vision. No other person has your kind of vision and nobody can achieve what you have been created to do, you are fearfully and wonderfully made; you are peculiar and so is your vision. Your faith in your vision is a major ingredient that drives the vision: It gives you the possibility mentality to achieve your goal and see it come to pass. Most times the strength to carry on in the face of challenges and opposition lies deep in your conviction which is embedded in your faith in the task ahead.

In Genesis 6:1, the scripture tells us a story of a people who were determined to build a tower that would reach the sky. They began to build and do what no other person had done before. They would have succeeded had not God intercepted their vision because it was contrary to His purpose for mankind. Two main factors accounted for their success:

(1)   They were united in purpose and
(2)   They believed in their dream

Nothing can stand in the way of a man who believes in his vision, no army in this world, no devil in hell, and no decree of opposition can stop him. Every adversary becomes an energy booster. The more the challenge is, the more the doggedness to continue in the pursuit of the vision. No man ever succeeded in accomplishing anything worthwhile who did not believe in that thing from the onset.

The first Africa – American USA president – Barack H. Obama during his campaign for his presidential election in 2008 had a slogan that became synonymous with him and his campaign – "yes we can – the change we believe in" he got the vote of American's because they saw a man who believed in his vision of change and he succeeded in convincing not only the nation of America but the entire world. That is the effect of one's beliefs one's vision. "Your faith in your vision is a major ingredient that drives the vision".

(C): CELEBRATE AND CONCENTRATE ON YOUR VISION: The way you carry on with your vision will tell a lot about you and the vision. If you believe in your vision, you will celebrate it. To celebrate your vision means to be enthusiastic about it and make it a song in your mouth. It becomes a tonic that keeps you, it is the air that you breathe and everything in your life revolves around it. Whenever anyone comes in contact with you, your vision becomes obvious from the very first encounter. They name you with your vision to the extent that it even replaces your real name.

In addition to celebrating your vision, the best safeguard to a vision is avoidance of distraction. Distraction drains a man's strength and renders him weak and incapacitated. A man who dumps his vision for another simply because there is a new thinking around will jump from one position to another. The Bible calls him an unstable man who is easily tossed here and there. It concluded that such a man cannot receive anything from God. Distraction is a "masked" thief of vision. Once it comes to play, it destroys every element and ruins the whole essence of the vision.

Concentrate on your vision and pay attention to it and you will succeed. Make it the focus of all your energies and resources and you will inevitably see the fruits of your labour. Make all efforts to stay on course in the pursuit of your dreams. Many are the distractions on the road of destiny; the wise avoid them and fix their attention on the job to be done.

One of the strategies of the enemy of vision is to make you lose concentration. No matter how well a man is doing on a job once he loses focus, he begins to fumble and will eventually fail. You cannot afford to lose concentration and get distracted if you must fulfil your vision. Determine to stay on track "The best safeguard to vision is the avoidance of distraction".

(D): DEVELOP AND DEFEND YOUR VISION: Develop your vision until it becomes big enough to accommodate your entire God given potential. The fulfilment of your purpose in life is determined by the vision you can dream of. Until you can see the bigger picture, God has for you, you may leave below your potentials. Vision is the gateway to that which he has for you.

The major difference between a vision and a goal is that while a goal is a destination, a vision is a means to an end and not an end itself. It is a window into the future, always pointing to the way to go. Because the level of your vision is tied to your level of insight. The higher your insight therefore, the higher your vision will be. Develop your vision by increasing your knowledge base of the Word by increasing your interaction with people that have gone ahead of you and drawing inspiration from them. Vision has the ability to grow from whatever level it is now; it only requires cultivation and dressing. Develop and dress your vision. Joseph started as a dreamer and he developed that gift until he became an interpreter of dreams. If he had remained as a dreamer, he might not have gotten to his God-given destiny. So develop, cultivate and dress your vision today and it will announce you soonest.

Another important thing to do with vision is to define it. Defend your vision against all foes. Beware of "vision stoppers".

Anything that can stop your vision can stop you. Be careful with whom you share your vision with. As many you run to for counsel may end up cancelling the vision, subtly they make nonsense of your dreams, they tell you, you cannot and if you believe them; it marks the end of your lofty aspirations. Be ready to shed your blood if need be to protect your God-given dream. It is better to die for something you believe in than to live and stand up for nothing. The history of South Africa and the end of apartheid will not be complete without the mention of Nelson Mandela. He stood for his vision, was jailed for life after being accused of sabotage, treason and violent conspiracy against the then government. He never stopped pushing for the vision of a free South Africa where every black person would be given equal opportunity as their white counterparts even from behind the bars. He later became the first black president of the country and won the Nobel Prize in 1993 for his perseverance and the defence of his vision. History books are filled with other great men and women who lost homes, jobs and even precious lives in the fight for their vision. The blood that these men and women shed have become like rain and dew that wet the fulfilment of their dreams. Stand up and defend our vision today and history will remember you long after you have gone.

(E): ENTHRONE YOUR VISION

"For I speak to you gentiles in as much as I am the apostle of the gentiles, I magnify mine office" – Romans 11 v 13.

Make your vision the biggest influence in your life only next to God. Every other thing in your life should be secondary to your vision if you must achieve your dreams. Let nothing contend with whatever vision you believe in. Relegate all other influences to the background; you can do without them. A lot of "legitimate" issues will be contending with your vision for your attention and resources. Do not deceive yourself that you can satisfy all of them. Your resources are limited and your time is fixed in a day. You can do certain things well enough for commendations, so don't waste the limited resources you have trying to meet all obligations.

In Mathew 6:33, Jesus said "seek ye first the kingdom of God and His righteousness and every other thing shall be added unto you" the statement has reverberated through human history and laid the foundation for this truth. It goes to mean that there are always first things to do and other issues of life just simply fall in line.

One of the first things in your life is your vision. In your scale of preference/priority, your vision should be at the top. Only then can it command the necessary attention it requires. "In your scale of preference/priority, your vision should be at the top".

(F): FOLLOW THROUGH WITH YOUR VISION: Don't give up on your vision no matter what: follow it through. No matter the obstacles, stick to it no matter how many times you have failed, stay by it and you will see it through. The vision is but for an appointed time! You must learn to hold on and to follow your heart when it bothers on your vision.

Abraham Lincoln (1809 – 1865) – the 16th president of the United States of America lost all elections he contested for before he won that of the office of the president. He simply followed his vision to the end and today years after, he is a legend and folk hero of American history. You cannot imagine what scorn he had to deal with during these trying periods of his life. Many would have written him off simply because he had failed before. Listen, failure is not final and should not deter you from following through with your vision. The longer it takes to get to your place in destiny, the sweeter the victory song. The bitter the experiences are, the better the testimony. The more risky the adventure is, the greater the reward. Vision fulfilment is not for the chicken-hearted, it is for men and women who will not turn back after putting their hands to the plow.

Beginners are not the ones that wear the crown but they that endure to the end. Your hands have started the vision; let your hands also finish it. The race is not necessary for the swift but for the finisher. For the accomplishment of your dreams, you need a strong "stay-power" to push to the end. "The longer it takes to get to your destiny, the sweeter the victory song".

(G): GO FOR GOLD: Go for your vision; go for gold, gold is one of the most precious and highly valued metallic elements. It is a soft, heavy, corrosion-resistant metal found in underground veins and alluvial deposits. It finds its way to palaces and it's worn only by princess and the rich. However, to gain access to this metal requires digging deep into the inner surfaces of the earth, going through the refining processes before it finally assumes the status of valuable commodity. The same is through for vision. Pursue your vision as a gold miner goes after his gold. Apostle Paul said "this one thing I do, forgetting the past I press for the mark of the high calling in Christ" – Philippians 3 v 14. Little wonder at the end of his ministry, he was bold to say he had finished the race and there laid for him in heaven a crown of glory. This is the attitude! All through his ministry, he always sought for the best, for the master and the church of God simply put, he went for gold. They that go for gold here on earth receive crowns of glory yonder. The world is waiting to celebrate your success and celebrate you. Make sure when the history of your generation would be written, your name will be entered in gold. Never hold back on the demand of the vision; be willing to pay the sacrifice no matter what. That is the attitude of vision accomplishers. "Pursue your vision as a gold miner goes after his gold".

(H): HAVE A VISION: This is the first commandment without which nothing else matters. You may have inherited a fortune but without vision, you will soon become a beggar. On the other hand, if you were not born with a silver spoon in your mouth; the only way to break the cycle of poverty is to have a vision. Vision is a motivator, an energizer and the drive behind every success in life. A vision is so powerful, while the lack of it is perilous. The prodigal son in Luke 11 asked his father for the portion of his inheritance that fell on him. The father was reluctant to give him not because he wanted to deny him his legitimate birth right, but paradventure he knew his son was a man without a vision. He was sad because he knew his son would waste all his hard-earned wealth recklessly. True to type, in a few years, the prodigal son became roommates with pigs, he was feeding from the leftovers, to keep body and soul together. Indeed, without vision, you become a waste of resources.

His father having known the kind of son he had, was waiting everyday outside his balcony for his return. He was glad when he saw him from afar of though looking untidy and emaciated. He nevertheless ran to embrace him. He was glad that he was still alive and secondly, that he had a second chance to teach him to have a vision for his life. He not only suffered loss of his inheritance but, he tasted the other side of life as a result of his vision-less-ness.

Africa is a continent though blessed with numerous natural resources abounding all across its lands but has been impoverished by the death of visionary leaders. These are leaders who have no single clue on what to do with its wealth and as a result, the continent has remained at the bottom of the ladder among the committee of nations. There is a search for men and women of vision to take Africa to the next level, to restore the hope and yearnings of its people to fulfil God's plan in these end times.

Romans 8 v 19 says "the earnest expectation of the creature waiteth for the manifestation of the sons of God "sons of God with vision and clarity of purpose, men who understand times and seasons and what we should be doing just like the sons of Issachar of old. Are you the one we are waiting for? Are you the man or woman who will lead the church of Jesus back to her master and Lord? Then be a man of vision. The prayer every man should pray irrespective of race or colour, status, or age therefore is Lord give me a vision for life. It should be sought for as if your life depends on it. It should top your prayer requests on a daily basis. No prayer or desire should be greater than that for vision. This is how important getting a vision is! "Vision is a motivator, an energizer and the drive behind every success in life".

(I): ISSOLATE NOT YOUR VISION FROM GOD: Your vision is a part of the big picture God has in mind for your life. You cannot isolate your vision from God's plan and purpose for your life and expect to succeed. Align your vision with God's Word; that way, you will never go astray. Some have made a ship wreck of their lives by claiming to have visions that clearly contradicts godliness.

The Bible says some ask / desire and have not; (James 1) they work hard and even deny themselves of food and comfort and yet live in lack. The reason is, they ask and desire these things for their personal aggrandizement and pride. There is no place for God's glory in all they envisage for life. They have isolated their vision from the source of all good things. What they get is utter frustration and piercing of their souls with sorrow.

Your vision no matter what it is must draw you closer to your creator and enhance God's plan for your life. The scripture states in proverbs 10 v 22 unequivocally that "The blessings of the Lord maketh rich and added no sorrow to it". The acid test for any vision is to answer the questions in the affirmative. Does it glorify God? Does it promote godliness? And does it draw you closer to God? If the answer to these questions is yes then, you are on the right track.

Many have come to wealth they were not prepared to manage and have made shipwreck of their faith. Others attained stardom and fame and allowed pride to puncture their very bright future. Any vision not in line with the Lord's purpose for your life must be cancelled "Your vision no matter what it must draw you closer to your creator and enhance God's plan for your life".

(J): JOIN HANDS WITH OTHERS: Two are better than one, because they have a good reward for their labour: for if one fall, the one will lift up his fellow but woe to him who is alone when he falls and has not another to lift him up "Ecclesiastes 4 v 9". As you pursue your God-given vision, there are vision helpers sent to give you assistance. These are those who will give you the necessary push you need and there are others who will raise your hands up when they grow weak. Two people who are agreeable on a matter have unlimited power at their disposal to actualize their dreams. This power is called the power of agreement established by the Lord Himself. He said anything two of you agree together on earth shall be done. (Mathew 18 v 19).

Jesus during His earthly ministry sought out twelve "vision helpers" – the twelve disciples. These men having caught his vision gave their lives and all for the fulfilment of the vision. They went everywhere propagating the message of salvation in His name. Christianity as it is today is the outcome of the relentless work of these great vision helpers. If Jesus could not do it alone though He was God in human form, how much less can you fulfill yours all by yourself? A man of vision is a leader of a kind; he gathers men and women of like minds and shares his vision with them and assigns tasks to each member of his team. Together the team under the leadership of the visionary gets the job done. Seek out your own vision helpers if you really desire to make it and align with them. Nobody is an island; remember, you need people who believe in you and your vision and who are ready to stake all to see the vision accomplished.

Members of a team play different roles for the overall good of the team. Some will provide the necessary link with the right person, while others will provide the finances needed for the execution of the project. Ignore your vision-helpers at your own risk. Some of the advantages of getting others involved in your vision are: you are stronger together, you share risks and burden and you have a good reward of your labour. "You need people who believe in you and your vision".

(K): KNOW YOUR VISION INSIDE OUT: "The labour of the foolish wearieth everyone because he knoweth not how to go to the city" – Ecclesiastes 10 v 15.

Knowledge is very vital in the issue of vision. There is no room for ambiguity. You have to be doubly sure,. A vision you do not know well or feel certain about, cannot carry the power of accomplishment. It takes certainty to ensure focus in the drive for vision. A destination you are not sure of, you will either not get there or lose direction along the way. What a tragedy! Joseph knew his dreams so well that he gave a very vivid description of them to his brothers and parents. He did not miss words when he told everyone he was to be their Lord. Although he could not see the path through the pit and the prison, but he knew his destination quite well. He knew the pit was not what he saw in his dreams, neither did the condition in the prison in any way resemble the affluence of the palace. He persevered because he knew where he was heading to. Until you are crystal clear about your vision, you will settle for less. You will accept whatever life throws at you and deprive yourself of the glory you were born to exhibit. You will become a burden to your world instead of being the much-awaited solution. Friends and family will scarcely relate with you because you do not know your direction in life. Vision carries with it the prize of acquiring knowledge. The scripture says in proverbs 23 v 23 "buy the truth and sell it not" read all you can about your dream and thereby empowering yourself for the challenges ahead. Arm yourself with current developments in the area of your vision, know what you require to achieve your goals. A student who desires to excel in his studies will first of all inquire what things he is expected to know and how to access the information. A builder will first sit down and find out what he requires to build the mansion of his dream. You cannot afford to accommodate ignorance at any level in the pursuit of your vision. "Until you are crystal clear about your vision, you will settle for less".

(L): LIMIT NOT THE POWER OF YOUR VISION: Vision has the power to influence, affect and impact lives; use it to the full. You can become anything you want to be, you can reach the top of your career, and you touch the sky. There is no limit for the man with a vision. The opportunities are in-exhaustive and the privileges are almost without an end. It is the power of vision that motivated the master to ignore the shame of the cross and the sufferings therein. The Bible says He endured pains because He had a vision of bringing many sons unto glory. It is also the power of vision that motivated a mountain climber to brave unfriendly winds and hazardous trails to reach the top of the mountain. It is the power of vision that makes an athlete train under the most unfavourable weather to become a world champion.

Like it has been said before, vision is an energizer, it gives you strength to carry on even when nothing else looks favourable. Do not undermine the power of your vision. Whether you are presently "a-nobody" in the eyes of the world or you are faced with major calamities in your past your vision will take you above all. It is not time to give up; rather it is time to mount up with wings like wings as an eagle. Dust off your coat, wipe those tears from your eyes and begin to dream again. It is time to believe again. You can, you will and you must "vision has the power to influence, affect and impact your life".

(M): MONITOR YOUR VISION: There must be monitoring parameters to constantly inform you on the performance of your vision. A monitor is a device that warns you of impending danger and alerts one to action. A vision without a monitor therefore will hit the rocks sooner or later. Because of the possibility of distraction, a "vision-monitor" becomes a necessary tool to possess as you embark on achieving your goal. For instance, a man who wants to lose weight must ensure he has a weighing scale to monitor his performance or else he may end up gaining more than he started out with. A business man who desires to grow a multi-national business empire must incorporate a way of monitoring his performance. It is your responsibility to check your monitor from time to time to guide you on the next step to take.

Your monitor tells you how well you are doing and whether you need to add or change your strategy. You cannot be doing the same thing over and over again and expect a change. The change you need to make in order to enhance your vision is informed by what you are seeing on your monitor when your monitor beeps red, you know it is time to stop or pause. It is time to take an inventory and correct whatever is out of place. Not a few visions have derailed from their original course. Quite a number have suffered premature death, all because there was no vision-monitor to alert when things began to go wrong. If you don't want your vision to end abruptly, go make yourself a monitor now. An example of a vision monitor is called a vision board. We shall look more at this at a later chapter of this book. "For you do not want your vision to end abruptly, go make yourself a monitor now".

(N): NEVER SAY NEVER: The word "never" does not exist in the dictionary of a man with vision. Instead of seeing the impossibilities, he seeks out other ways of accomplishing the task. Anything is possible for a man with vision, the vision-man says why not. Never means: "Negative effect against vision verily enslaves the result "Anywhere the word never is accommodated in the pursuit of vision, it enslaves and hinders result. You cannot achieve anything when you allow your mind to be fixed on what others have said that you can't do it. Maybe you grew up in an atmosphere where you have been constantly told you can never amount to anything good: it's time for you to prove them wrong. Do not allow people who do not know what God has deposited and created in you to limit you.

In verse 7 of Genesis 21, Sarah after the Lord had answered her and opened her womb, said "God hath made me to laugh who would have said to Abraham that Sarah should have given children suck? For I have born him a son in his old age "Sarah gave birth to Isaac at a time when it was said she could never have a child. She was a "write-off" by all standards both medical and otherwise. She eventually proved that the word "never" does not exist in the life of a man who believes in God. What is it that you have been told you cannot do or become? In what ways have you been written off or have you written yourself off? There is no faculty or department where a first-class honour is not possible; it only takes a man of vision to prove it. There is no situation that will never change. You can achieve your goal and never allow "never" to enslave your reward in God. "You cannot achieve anything when you allow your mind to be fixed on what others have told you that you cannot do IT".

(O): OPEN YOUR VISION TO CRITICISM: Critics are our unpaid teachers; don't be scared of them. A visionary man brings his ideas and hypothesis to be criticized by other people. He knows that the criticism of others will only bring out the best in his vision. The more they criticize your vision, the better it becomes and it also shows, you have something that stimulates interests from people. Gamaliel – a Pharisees and a teacher of the law rose among the Sanhedrin during the persecution of the early apostles and said "refrain from these men and let them alone" for if the counsel or work be of men, it will come to naught: but if it be God, ye cannot overthrow it; lest ye be found fighting against God (Acts 5 v 34-39). Every vision because it is new will attract criticism and opposition, however if it be of God, it will defer every whims and skims of men. The more they criticize, the more the vision expands and grows under His watchful eyes. Criticism has many advantages if taken well. One of these advantages includes improvement of your vision. When someone criticizes your dreams, it gives you room and opportunity to improve on the areas of deficiencies. Secondly, it gives you a sense of responsibility to prove that what you have is genuine. You will do all it takes to ensure your dream sees the light of the day. Without criticism, many a vision would be inadequate defiant and lack bite.

(P): PROMOTE YOUR VISION: The best commodities will rust away without proper promotion and marketing. Promote your vision with your mouth, the way you look and the way you do things. Let the world know the deposit inside you – you are a solution to a problem. Promote your vision now and it will promote you later. The other word for the promotion of visions is called manifest.

It is declaring the things you dream of and your aspirations for life. Vision promotion determines how far your vision will go and its impact on your world. Nobody will know what you are capable of until you manifest it. Until Joseph offered to interpret the dream of the butler and the baker in prison, nobody knew he had such ability. In a way he promoted his vision by interpreting those dreams that night and when king pharaoh needed a dream interpreter, he was sent for. That was how the dream he had as a seventeen-year-old boy came to pass. If he had kept quite when the opportunity to promote his vision came along, he might have spent longer years in prison and maybe he might not have had his dream realized. Opportunities to promote or enhance your vision will always show up here and there in your life. They could come in different ways and forms but they will always come. Do you have the vision of becoming a great preacher? The opportunity to show what you have inside presents itself when you are asked to lead a Sunday school or exhort a house fellowship in your area. How will you prepare for it and how will you execute these assignments may be your vision-launcher?

Whatever your dreams are, you will often find opportunities to promote these or those dreams. Do not miss out on the chance to make your vision come through. Above all else, the best way to promote your vision is to commit it unto God's hand every day in the place of prayer. Praying for your visions and dreams is like oiling the vision against friction and opposition from man and the devil. The Bible says "Commit thy ways unto the hands of God and he shall direct thy paths". The place of prayer in the fulfilment of vision cannot be over-emphasized. Apart from pouring oil on your vision, your vision will receive direction and you also receive power to pursue it to accomplishment. "Opportunities to promote or enhance your vision will always show up here and there in your life".

(Q): QUESTION YOUR VISION: How sound is your idea to yourself? Until you are able to convince yourself about the soundness of your vision and its feasibility, you are very far from making it a reality before another individual will believe in your vision enough to show commitment, it must be sound enough. Your visions appeal resides in its soundness. Paul got to a point in his ministry that he queried his own calling. Different people had questioned his authority in the Church and almost eroded his influence over them. However, in Romans 9 v 1-2, he asked this question "Am I not an Apostle"? Am I not free? Have I not seen Jesus Christ our Lord? Are not ye my work in the Lord? If I be not an apostle unto others, yet doubters I am to you. For the seal of mine apostleship are ye in the Lord "he went ahead to establish the authenticity of his calling in the latter verses of the chapter.

When you are able to raise and answer questions about your vision, you succeed in stopping the mouth of gain-sayers be sure of this very fact that many will disagree with you and your vision; others will disagree with your methodology and approach. It is not new, every great vision has received and will continue to receive criticism and your only antidote is your being sure of what you are doing from the onset "when you are able to raise and answer questions about your vision, you succeed in stopping the mouth of gain-sayers".

(R): REVISIT AND RE-ASSESS YOUR VISION; UPDATE YOUR VISION REGULARLY

Don't belong to the stone-age. Vision is not static nor is it final. You must re-visit your vision to assess its relevance and its work ability in the light of unfolding circumstances. As knowledge increases and access to information enlarges, your vision needs regular re-assessment. Re-assessment of your vision is also important to help guide the course of doing the things you should be doing. Every vision should have a score board where it is regularly assessed. Different scores are awarded and the scores graded to enable you have an overall evaluation of what you are engaged in. A Leader or a politician should have a score board where his electoral promises are weighed alongside his performance. A student should have his/her score board to evaluate his/her progress in school. A pastor who is passionate about growing a strong and viable Church should develop a score board for his own perusal. No matter what your vision is and what you are involved in, one of the ways to regularly revisit or re-assess yourself is to score your performance. Grade it into excellent, very good, good, poor and very poor.

(S): SHARE YOUR VISION AND BE SPECIFIC: Great men with vision are not afraid to tell others what their dreams and visions are. They are proud to be associated with great ideas! Don't be afraid to share your vision. Be bold enough to let others hear what you are incubating in your great mind. Some people have felt that sharing their vision with others will expose them to unnecessary attacks and bad blood. People have cited the example of Joseph saying he went through so much hardship and hatred from his brothers because he shared his dream with them. True as this may seem, it is not enough to keep your mouth shut concerning your vision, only be discrete with it. Sharing your vision has two advantages namely: people will contribute resources to the fulfilment of the vision they believe in and they will also serve as your vision monitors. From what we have established earlier in this chapter, you need other people (vision helpers) to fulfil your vision. Some have the resources you do not have, while others may have the connections you do not possess. There are foundations all over the world ready to fund projects and ideas that will impact positively on mankind. How will they get to know you have got something we all need if you do not share that dream/vision?

Specificity of vision is paramount to vision fulfilment. You cannot allow ambiguity when it comes to vision. It must be specific, direct to the point and straight forward. You ask some people what their vision is all about and what you hear is a collection of confabulations of words. Others have so many complexities in their vision that is so difficult to delineate exactly what their vision is. Your vision must be conveyed in a vision-statement, reproducible and devoid of uncertainty.

"Be bold enough to let others hear what you are incubating in your great mind".

(T) TIME YOUR VISION; IT PAYS: "TO EVERYTHING THERE IS A SEASON, AND A TIME TO EVERY PURPOSE UNDER THE HEAVENS" – Ecclesiastes 3 v 1: Tie energy of your vision to a time frame. Every vision has its time and season both in terms of relevance and fulfilment. You should have a long term and short-term vision. It could be hourly basis, weekly even yearly. Once one vision is accomplished, another begins. Any vision left hanging without a time allocation will never be realized. An example of tying your vision to a particular time frame is illustrated below. A young man whose dreams of becoming the Nations president someday will do well by having a time-table of his political ambition. By certain periods in life, he shall set goals and vision to be met at specific times in his political journey. You can almost tell how far an individual will go by what he has achieved in a space of time. There is a saying if you are not rich by age forty, you may as well forgo being rich. Though not an absolute statement, it does carry with a lot of wisdom to learn from "any vision left hanging without a time allocation will never be realized".

(U): USE YOUR GIFT: Neglect not the gift that is in thee – 1 Timothy 4 v 14: your gift is the gateway to your vision fulfilment. Little wonder the Bible says that the gift of a man will make room for him. Where vision is concerned, put your best foot first. You have a gift that will help ensure the accomplishment of your vision. Every gift is tied towards a vision fulfilment! Whatever your area of gifting is that is the clue to your placement in life. It is difficult to see a man excel above the level of his talents/gifts. There are footballers who came into the beautiful game by sheer hard work and interest. There is a limit to which they can go in the game. However, there are natural, talented players and their mastery of the game leaves no one in doubt. These are those that achieve stardom without such ado. David had the opportunity of staying in the palace of King Saul ever before he was chosen to be king by simply using his musical gift. The king needed somebody who was skilful on the keyboard to calm him down. David's gift came handy and played so well that the king fell in love with him. No doubt your gift will speed up your vision. Undoubtedly, Apostle Paul understood this principle when he was telling Timothy to stir up the gift in him. I want to at this juncture charge you also to begin to stir up your gift because as you do so, you invariably speed up your vision. "You have got a gift that will help ensure the accomplishment of your vision".

(V): VISUALIZE YOUR VISION ON A DAILY BASIS: Never remove your vision from your sight. As you behold your vision that is what you become because you will ultimately become what you behold. As you visualize your vision and meditate on it, you shall make your vision prosperous. One way to visualize your vision is by creating your vision board, your vision board should contain in explicit format the details of your vision statement; just the way you want to be in real life experience. Secondly, hang your vision board on a very conspicuous location in your room for you to see it daily. Vision board shall be discussed in greater details in the chapter – the concept of vision board. "As you behold your vision that is what you will become because you ultimately become what you behold".

(W): WRITE DOWN YOUR VISION AND MAKE IT PLAIN: "Write the vision and make it plain upon tables – Habakkuk 2 v 2. This is a golden rule. What you have not written down, you shall forget and what you forget, you cannot achieve. Jesus said concerning His vision; "as it is written concerning Me, I have come to do thy will O Lord" remember the smallest of pens is better than the best of brains. Writing down your vision has more than one advantage. The process of writing involves every part of your senses i.e. the brain, the eyes, your hands etc. this brings all your faculties to bear on a singular task. This way, your vision succeeds. Further generations, generations unborn can have access to your thoughts and ideas and par-adventure improve on them. Don't allow your dreams and visions to end with you, put your pen to paper right now and imprint your vision on the marbles of time. "What you have not written down, you will forget and what you forget, you cannot achieve".

(Y) YES, YOU CAN: "I CAN DO ALL THINGS THROUGH CHRIST WHO GIVES ME STRENGTH" Philippians4 v 13.

You can do all things by simply having a vision of it. It is time to say yes to all your dreams. Saying yes means you agree with the fact that you can do it; it also means that you are what God says you are. From the onset, you must realize that you are nothing without the grace and enablement of the Lord. However, with God you can do the unimaginable, the unthinkable because you are resting and trusting in His unfailing power. Always remind yourself that you can do all things through Christ who gives us strength. Know this dearly beloved, no one can truly claim to achieve anything by the strength of His arms, for by strength shall no man prevail. Paul did so much and even labour more than the apostles before him but his summary was "I can do all things through Christ who gives me strength". Indeed, you can!

(Z) Zero all obstacles from beginning

No vision comes easy or cheap; therefore, zero your mind towards all hindrances, ignore them and concentrate on what you have to do when you have made up your mind that opposition and difficulty will not deter you from reaching your goal, then you are ready for the challenges ahead. Apostle Paul in Acts 20 v 24; said "none of these things move me" what a statement to make in the pursuit of one's vision! Different things will come to move you from the direction of your vision, but you must zero them in your mind before they zero your vision. The mind is the place where all battles are fought and winning or losing the battle depends on your mind-set. Overcome all opposition in your mind if you must climb to the top of your vision. Life will only give you what you demand for and not what is your due. "Overcome all opposition in your mind if you must climb to the top of your vision".

Chapter Four

Developing Mental Attitude

"You Will Never Change Your Actions, Until You Change Your Mind Set"

Mental Attitude: This is the basic way we carry out our thinking, believing, desires, habits, motives, talking, behaviour and actions in life. It is either positive or negative in nature but it depends on one's choice and the decision he or she exercises with the kind and sources of information used by such an individual in life. It is fear; ignorance and greed that affect human beings that produce negative attitudes. Attitude, one's beliefs and environment; helps to describe human life. When you want to convert an inferior fellow to a superior person, that inferior fellow will need to possess these virtues: desire, enthusiasm and persistence in life. If any person wants to attain excellence in life, he needs these attributes: self-discipline, sacrifice and a fighting spirit. In order to make this chapter of developing mental attitude on both side (positive or negative), we need to deal with it effectively to get to the meaning of mental attitude in human existence, so that one can possibly know what he or she should stick to and those areas he or she must completely avoid in life.

Positive mental attitude is the answer to everything in life while negative mental attitude is a question mark in any person or person's existence. Build yourself as a solution and not as a problem. Always make sure you know what you are allowing inside your mind and what you are disallowing from your mind, so as to build a successful existence. The choice is yours. Whatsoever you chose now will determine you and your family's future. So be wise, be smart and be bold to take the right decisions to make a difference in your generation. By making things to happen positively. You need to focus on the positive side of mental attitude because that will give you the beauty of life and help to influence the lives of others. Positive attitude is the foundation of success in any field of endeavour.

The quickest way to develop positive mental attitude is to do things now; not delaying or wasting time or procrastinating but doing it immediately or acting promptly. Also, the fastest way to develop positive self-esteem is to help others that can't pay you back in cash or kind in life.

Total quality people are those people that sharply possess these attributes – character, integrity, positive attitudes and good values in life.

Factors That Determines Attitudes

These are three – called: the three E's

(1)   ENVIRONMENT
(2)   (2) EDUCATION
(3)   (3) EXPERIENCE

ENVIRONMENT: This aspect of the factor that determines one's attitude or behaviour in life has been classified into these forms: Culture and social background, traditional beliefs, political and economic environments. These factors come from the environmental aspect of a living man, but with positive mental attitude, one can possibly control his or her favoured or unfavourable environmental factors in life. Confront your situations with a right attitude not with wrong attitude to attain success in life.

EDUCATION: This aspect describes one's mental product or state which really regulates one's mind-set which will bring about how to utilize one's mind and time in life. If your educational level is low then the possibility to have right judgment in life will be difficult unlike a sound educated person/people. Know that a reader of today will always be the leader of tomorrow. As reading is to the mind that is how exercise is to the body.

Reading makes a man, while writing exalts a man. If you think education is expensive then try ignorance. You can really measure your mental power and strength of education by the height of knowledge acquired in life. All you need is to invest into your mind, soul, time, strength and resources (human, material) through education, it pays greatly in life. But personal development strategies make the real difference in life. Always be prepared to enrich your brain power or mental strength; it defines your real values in existence. Go for it with all your vigour, determination and great commitment.

EXPERIENCE: As the old saying goes; experience is the greatest teacher. That is the naked truth of man's existence you need to learn from past mistakes. Don't repeat the same mistake in the near future. Build your mind to learn two things from your mistakes, know the wrong way of doing it and the opportunities given to think out another way. To do it again and an experience tells you what to do while confidence allows you do it better. Many people are controlled by negative experience of the past because they lack positive mental attitude and good values or the right mind-set. They always have the past experience (negatively) right at their front blocking them from seeing the future. "now is not the time to put blames unto the past but to put a cause for the future" – John F. Kennedy.

For instance, we (my daddy's children) grew up to know that cats are wicked or evil, we ran from them because we looked at them as destroyers especially at night; which is not really the truth. Most people's past experience regulates their existence. Know that experience is that activity or happening that has come into your life, while one is living within a given environment from his or her childhood to adulthood; it can be positive or negative experience but checkmate them with the use of God's Word and gather the right information about such experiences, so that one can't live under the threat of fear, doubts and discouragements.

James Williams a professor researcher and philosopher with Harvard University USA, said – 85% of any person's success lies on his attitude, while the remaining 15% are just facts and figures. He discovered that man can alter his life by altering the attitude of his mind (James Williams). He went further to say that – man has not failed in life because he basically lacks these five d's: direction, desire, discipline, dedication and determination in life.

HOW TO BUILD POSITIVE MENTAL ATTITUDES

These are possible factors that help any person to build a positive mental attitude in life. They are as follows:

(1)   Change your focus, look out for positive things; try to picture opportunities in any given circumstance or situation and see the best in others in life. Concentrate on the positive side of existence.

(2)   Make a habit of doing things now, not procrastinating or delaying but do it immediately, or applying prompt action in life. After you might have gotten an idea turn it into action. James Williams said – if you want any great accomplishment, learn how to do things immediately. Also, Scott Witt said: reasons why people are failures is not lack of ability, knowledge, ideas and know how; but lack of action.

(3)   Developing an attitude of gratitude is a power of appreciation and recognition in life. Those that appreciate or give thanks for smaller gift will always prepare to receive greater gifts in the future. Only a cheerful heart receives a bigger gift in life. Those that possess a heart of appreciation attracts greater favours and blessings in their existence. Just keep on appreciating, you will get surprises.

(4)   Get into a continued education programme; it is a singular act that helps to build one's mind which will help to

open greater opportunities and possibilities of seeing into the future for a better day to come. It is the strategy of building the inner man(mind) by embracing life time learning which is an express pathway to a greater and brighter future in life.

(5)   Building a positive self-esteem is the best way you can feel positive from the inside. People with positive self-esteem possess self-confidence, self-control, externally driven, playing it smartly, good values and positive mental attitude to life. They believe in cause and effect, not in luck or possessing fatalistic attitude.

(6)   Stay away from negative influence; this destructive act has been an old negative attribute that have befallen the youths and adults alike. In every relationship contracted, it is either positive or negative, but the attributes produced from every existing relationship testify the kind of it, in a given settling, the kind of

association or friends you keep greatly tell the kind of person you are in life. This toxic relationship or people exist in every part of the world no matter the height of its development or civilization; the evil minded people exist in any given place or areas on the surface of the earth. If you have the right mind-set then you will know the kind of people you hang out with or keep as friends, because they describe your attitude or behaviour easily in life. Charles Jones said: there are two things that help to build one's wisdom, the books you read and the kind of people you keep. You have to keep people with a right mind-set and avoid negative minded fellows that have a wrong mind-set in life. (7)   Learn to do those things that need to be done rightly. This clearly makes a person to have a positive attitude, being the person that rejoices over positive activities and godly attributes. They wish to associate with excellent things of great qualities and associate quickly with them without any element of delay. The act of associating one's life with excellence attracts excellence to one's life.

(8) Start your day with something positive: this helps in a great measure to improve and re-engineer the mind-set of a person such that he or she will be built positively as he or she chooses to do positive things first; things in the morning like waking up at midnight to pray and appreciate God and think positively, write down one's ideas and read great books. It will open the mind for positive and godly purpose for the new day. It is a weapon for capturing the new day for victorious and successful end in life. When you begin the day from the right side, you will bring unique things to existence.

(9) Develop the attitude of treating others positively: this step helps in building a person's self-esteem positively. There is joy in the heart of a generous

mind to help others. Robert Greene said that: only generous souls attain greatness in life. A man said you make your living from what you receive, but you will make life from what you give unto others. William Ward said that: the key to abundant life is caring about others, sharing with others and daring for others. You can't beat the power of helping others. Only the conscious sow and forget the reaping. Stop craving for what to gain; be conscious of what to invest or give out. Seeing opportunities in every given situation: this is an ability to see inward or the unseen in the strength to been creative and innovative in a given circumstance coupled with auto suggestion or the visualization to attain a great result in life. Those that live with their spiritual eyes or the inner eye picture abundance or unlimited things in life.

There are three kinds of people: the strong-minded people that talk about ideas or dreams, the average minded people that discuss events, while the small-minded people discuss people (others) and their affairs.

Three categories of people exist on the surface of the earth:

Those who make things happen

Those who watch things happen and

Those who ask what is happening.

And there are three kinds of people: those that are investors in life, those that are supportive in life, and those that are watchers in life.

You have to sincerely indicate where you belong to and check if it is lucrative, if yes then build upon it to associate with the successful group.

FEATURES OF POSITIVE MENTAL ATTITUDE

Here, we are talking about how a man can possibly attain success. You can only reach your successful goals with a positive attitude and not with negative attitudes or self-destructive behaviour or unsuccessful habits in life.

Louis IV said that: little will only be withheld from a man that has conquered himself. A man with right mental attitude attains greater success in life, while a man with a wrong mental attitude obtains a consummate failure in life.

These are clearly notable features of positive attitude: burning desire, determination, commitment, integrity, maturity, excellence, uniqueness, boldness, smartness, courage, intelligence, abundance, self-discipline, optimism, kindness, love, enthusiasm, hard work, persistence, focus, direction, deadline, fighting spirit, responsibility, prompt action, faithfulness, sincerity, gratitude, mind appreciation, honesty, goal setting, self-confidence, self-control, positive self-esteem and self-talk, consistence and right motives.

ATTRIBUTES OF POSITIVE MENTAL ATTITUDE

(1) They believe in cause and effect, sowing and reaping sustaining and abstaining, living in the world with principles.

(2) They possess strong mind or right mind-set in life

(3) They study great books to gather rich information about themselves, others and the environment they live in

(4) They don't compromise their integrity in life

(5) They basically know the kind of people they keep or associate with in life, they avoid toxic people

(6) They build a big picture in their mind while making decisions in life

(7) They know their weakness and smartly make correction where necessary

by converting their weakness into strength in order to put their existence in the winning circle

(8) They identify their strength and wisely build on them

(9) They pursue their goals with their brain power or mental strength not with physical strength or body power

They play to win and not to lose in life

(10) They live by faith and not by sight, they live by looking inward

(11) They chase after realities and not after shadows

(12) They know their purpose (mission in life) identify their potentials (talents) and recognize limitless opportunities and take advantage of them

(13) They live to influence the lives of others positively

(14) They build the house of trust in life

FEATURES OF NEGATIVE MENTAL ATTITUDE:

Destructive desires, destructive thoughts, wrong choices, wrong decisions, wrong motives, negative self-esteem, negative self-talk, bad habits, directionless, lack of confidence, purposelessness, doubts, fear, discouragement, ignorance, procrastination, distraction, believing in luck, idleness, laziness, greed, selfishness, enviousness, jealousy, hatred playing it safe, time wasting, wrong mind-set, gossiping, victim languages, bad experiences, questionable character, defensive, externally driven and blaming others for one's failure in life.

ATTRIBUTES OF NEGATIVE MENTAL ATTITUDE

1. They seek for security in life and then lives being insecure

2.   They pursue their goals with physical strength or body power

3.   They pursue shadows leaving the realities of life

4.   They are small minded or average minded people

5.   They are controlled by circumstances, events and environmental factors

6.   They are afraid to confront their challenges in life

7.   They give up easily or quit in life

8.   They believe in scarcity which makes greedy or selfish and which produces great fear in life

9.   They don't see opportunities in any given situation or circumstance

10.   They don't believe in others people's abilities in life

11.   They doubt themselves by building discouragement in their life

12.   They compete with others in life

13. They base their security upon the lives of others

14. They act without thinking

15. They completely refuse to learn anything in life

16. They lack vision, knowledge and prompt action in life

17. They pursue money for money not developing ideas to turn them unto action for money in life

18. They always look outside

19. They lack insight about issues and failure to see the future

20. They consider the past and remain in the present to forget their future

21. They play too much, sleep too much and eat too much

SIGNS OF GREAT ATTITUDE

1. Believe in yourself

2. Willingness to see the best in others

3.   Ability to see opportunities everywhere one finds himself

4.   Focus on solution

5.   Desire to give

6.   Persistence/determination

7.   Self-discipline and sacrifice

8.   Taking responsibilities for their lives and that of others

9.   Possessing these great virtues of life; love, patience and courage

10.   Embracing long life learning

11.   Embracing personal development strategies

12.   Confronting his or her fears, doubts and discouragements

13.   Possessing self-confidence and self-control

14.   Possessing the three greatest duties of mankind: unto God be faithful, unto yourself be sincere and unto others be truthful in life

15.   Developing ideas or dreams by turning them into actions in life

16.	Launching into one's invisible realm
17.	Always having fun in whatsoever you have chosen to do; put the first things first

YOU MAY SUCCEED IF NOBODY ELSE BELIEVE IN YOU, BUT YOU WILL NEVER SUCCEED IF YOU DO NOT BELIEVE IN YOURSELF

Chapter Four

Vision for Exploits

"Looking (Away from All That Will Distract) To Jesus - Hebrew 12:2"

In this chapter, we shall be looking at a very vital aspect of vision i.e. vision for exploits.

Having established the A-Z of vision, it becomes very imperative to address the nature of what we fix our gaze and pay attention to. What you are looking at per day has an unprecedented influence on you and your output in life. You attract what you envision; this is the law of attraction.

The scripture above says "looking away and looking unto" this is an incredible statement of truth. To properly assess the dividends of vision, we must be looking at the right thing all the time. Our attention should be focused on what we want to experience and not on the challenges we face. The scripture states uniquely that, there must be a looking away from all that distract before we can correctly look at what is appropriate. Things that distract are limitless and they range from problems and challenges to unpleasant life's experiences. Until you look away from that sickness and look at the provision of healing and good health as provided for in the scriptures, you may not be able to assess your healing.

Two outstanding characters one each from the Old Testament and the New Testament of the Holy Bible exemplify the effect of looking and seeing correctly.

ABRAHAM: Genesis 15 v 2 states "and Abram said, Lord God, what will Thou give me, seeing I go childless, and the steward of my house is this Eliezer of Damascus?

The entire scripture is filled with passages that reveal Abraham's stand with God. One of the profound statements on him is when the scripture refers to him as the friend of God. He has also been described as the Father of Faith. However, the above verse of scripture gives an insight into an important lesson for us from the life of this giant of Faith. After God had promised him a child, he got to a point in his life like many of us that his attention was drawn from the initial promise. All he could see at this period was his state of childlessness. As long as he was seeing childlessness, the promised child could not be born. Par-adventure, the delay he experienced was primarily a fallout of this very attitude. The more he was seeing his problem, the farther he was getting away from the promise. The performance of the promise depends on "seeing the promise".

Numbers 21:6-9 reveal another perspective to the relevance of looking and seeing what we ought to see. As a punishment to their murmuring in the wilderness, God sent fiery serpents to bite the children of Israel so that many people can die. After they repented and Moses prayed to God for them, the Lords solution was simple." Make thee a fiery serpent and set it upon a pole, that every one that is bitten when he looks upon it shall live."

The Lords provision was not just a simple glance at the serpent set upon the pole, purposeful and continuous look. Every man that was bitten by this fiery serpent had his deliverance in looking away from the pain of the bite and looking upon the fiery serpent set upon the pole. No matter how painful the bite was, he must ignore it and look away from it and then look up. Herein laid his salvation and deliverance

Is this an easy thing to do? Not at all. The situation is painful and choking and there seems to be no immediate way out of it. In the midst of all these, scriptural provision is that you look away from the situation, change your gaze and look up. The psalmist says I look up to the hill, from where my help cometh from, my help cometh from the Lord who made the heavens and the earth "the devil wants you to nurse the injury, but the Lord wants you to ignore it. In nursing the injury, you pay unnecessary attention to the devil which he wants, but you deny yourself from divine help. As many of the children of Israel that refused to pay attention to the pain of the bite but instead look upon the situation lived on the other hand, the Lot that concentrated on the pain and discomfort of the bite perished. Matthew 14:30 "But when he saw the wind boisterous, he was afraid and beginning to sink…" Peter took a step of faith and asked Jesus "Lord, if it be thou, bid me come unto to thee on the water." Immediately Jesus said come, and Peter jumped on the water and he began to walk on stormy water to the words of the master. As long as his gaze and attention was on the Lord, he remained a float on the water. Scripture did not tell us how long and how far Peter walked but imagine it was a quite a distance. Reason is because Jesus sent the disciples away and retired in the evening (6-9pm) to pray till the fourth watch(3-6am)when he began to walk on the water. However somewhere along the line for whatever reason, Peter lost his gaze and began to look at the waves of the sea instead of the master. He turned from the word and turned on the prevailing situation of the world. He suddenly realized he was walking on the same water that was contrary to their voyage and how he was drowned in the fear of it. The bible says he began to sink. Did the water suddenly become more powerful or more antagonistic? No! The explanation it is not far-fetched, He looked away from help and dwelled on the wave. Peter would have drowned to death had he not quickly cried out to Jesus and shouted for help…he cried, saying "Lord save me "immediately the Lord stretched forth his hands and saved him. He is the present help in times of trouble! The same water he had controlled over awhile earlier would have swallowed him just simply because he looked wrongly at the winds. Are you faced with a contrary wave that threatens to drown you? Is the wind blowing over you at the moment boisterous making you unsure whether you will get over to the other side? Hear me, you will walk on this troubled water to the other side of destiny in the mighty name Jesus Christ. All you need right now is to ignore the waves and the wind. The bible says "he that observes the wind will not sow" ignore the wind and look unto Jesus the author and finisher of your faith. As long as your gaze is fixed on him, your voyage is secured and you will have a safe landing on shore.

Outcome Of Looking At The Problem it Prevents The Birth Of The Promise

Looking at the problem will prevent the promise from getting fulfilled. As long as Abraham was seeing childlessness and Eliezer as heir, Isaac could not be born. When you are fixating on issues that bother you, there is no vacancy for the solution. Even when the answers eventually come, you cannot appreciate them because you are hooked on the problem. All the Israelites who flaunted the instruction of looking upon the "solution serpent" on the pole died even though the cure was a look away. The promise is only a look away from where you are right now. May the Lord help you change your gaze and fix on Jesus' name.

It Breeds Fear and Hence Drowning

The same Peter, who had acted in faith some moments earlier and walked on water, was so afraid for his life that he would drown. This is typical of what looking at the problem does even to the best of us. The Fear that the problem will kill you, that you will not make it and so on and so forth. All these are the result of paying unnecessary attention to one challenge. Nobody is saying the challenge is not a big one, I am not denying the fact that you have to stay long on this case but nursing the issue will only produce fear. Fear comes with its own torment and though there is only one problem initially, fear will produce many others because it has got" offspring, Look away for a moment from the problems and you will see your fear melt away like wax before the fire. The power is derived from making you stay on the problem, but once you ignore it, it loses its sting.

It Magnifies the Problem Beyond Proportion

The more you look at the problem, the more it gets magnified and it grows into a monster. The power of a challenge to grow is resident in the attention you give to it. This is because anything you pay attention to automatically grows. One of the worst aftermaths of paying attention to and thus magnifying a problem is that it gets to a point that it tends to dwarf the "bigness" of God in your sub-conscious. Whereas as you are praying for God to change the situation, meanwhile in your heart, the problem is bigger than what he can do,

It Offers an Alternative

Lastly, after looking at and concentrating on the problem for some time, alternative arrangement becomes the only feasible solution. It just follows naturally. Abraham had waited for the promised child for twenty years plus and he turned to an alternative, another way of getting the problem apparently solved.

The first alternative was Eliezer of Damascus. Abraham elevated a servant into the position of his heir in his heart. It is undoubtedly not his first choice of an heir but he had looked too long on his childlessness that a servant would do at this stage. Eliezer began to enjoy a little more favour them previously and he was enough. Madam Sarah vacated her place in the bedroom for a maid. After Hagar became pregnant and gave birth to Ishmael, Sarah became a maid in her own house: -a double dose of tragedy, as a result of seeing a problem rather than the promise. When you fixate on the problem, you permit abnormalities to prevail in your life. A servant will become heir and maid will become madam.

Chapter Five

The Exploits Of Vision

A vision is a powerful tool an individual arm himself with to secure his future. The power of vision refers to the effect, the influence, the impact and the control of vision. The power of vision is awesome. It can turn a seemingly weak man to a man of great strength and courage. A poor young man became one of the richest men in Nigeria through the power of vision. His name was M.K.O Abiola – the acclaimed winner of June 12 presidential election in Nigeria in 1993. Nothing can stand in the way of a man of vision;

everything gives way and answers to him. Your vision can have a profound influence on your life that you now come under its control.

Until your vision can affect and influence your life, it's no vision at all. A man's vision is greater than him because it controls the way he talks, behaves and controls every aspect of his life. An athlete cannot afford certain social behaviours if he has a vision of being the best. A student who desires to graduate with a first class from college will lead a regimented life as demanded by his vision. A family who has a building project for instance will avoid the other pleasures of unwise spending to be able to save towards that project. The list is endless; do you still doubt the power of vision? I hope not. However, if you discover that you are in control of your vision, you need to redefine that vision.

VISION PRESERVES!

The scriptures say that where there is no vision, the people perish. What a profound statement! A man without vision dies many times over at the slightest opposition. However, a visionary man sees challenges on his way as stepping stones to greater glory. When you are down and hard pressed, your vision becomes your source of strength to carry on. Vision keeps alive; you cannot die easy when your vision is alive. There is always something to live for, if you have a vision nothing preserves like vision.

Simeon in scripture (Luke 2:24-35) refused to die despite his old age simply because he had a vision of seeing the promised messiah. The day the child – Jesus was brought to the temple where he was for dedication, was the fulfilment of his long awaited vision. The vision kept him alive through his years of waiting. He said "now Lord you have kept your promise and you may let your servant go in peace, with my eyes I have seen your salvation which you have prepared in the presence of all people".

A woman went through series of life threatening surgeries to correct some surgical conditions. The surgical team not too sure of her pulling through anaesthesia and the surgeries and the outcome of these procedures could not be guaranteed, however she survived all the procedures how? She had the vision of returning into the recovery room to meet her husband who was waiting for her each time she had to go through the series of surgeries. A whole community was once saved by a group of sick folks because of the power of vision. 2 kings 7, they opined that to take their lives in their hands and go into the enemy's camp was better than staying put where they were. The result was that they not only survived but discovered abundance of food necessary to preserve a nation.

VISION PROPELS TO ACTION

Vision produces action! A man with a vision is a hardworking man. He does not laze around like the hinges of a door because he has goals and targets to meet. While others are rolling from one end of their bed to the other, he is mindful of the number of hours he must lay to sleep. He is seeing new grounds to conquer and new plans to develop.

He is a busy man, Apostle Paul told King Agrippa "where upon o King Agrippa, I was no disobedient unto the heavenly vision (acts 26 v 19). Your vision will bring you to a state of obedience. It makes you do its bidding no matter what the prize. According to his own testimony, Paul worked more than the other disciples in his ministry. He could not refrain even in the presence of threats and dangers to his own life. He was ready to die while carrying the vision he had received from the Lord. The major difference between day-dreaming and vision is that the day-dreamer does not put his hands to work while the man with a vision is propelled to action to see his vision through.

VISION PRODUCES ANDURANCE

Endurance is the ability to bear prolonged hardships and tolerate suffering. The road to accomplishment of vision often times is the road to hardship and unbearable suffering. A man with a vision possesses unusual tolerance towards harsh conditions. The vision keeps him going no matter what, one of the reasons Jesus endured so much pain and suffering from the hands of his creatures was His vision. From every stripe He received, He was seeing the joy of bringing many sons unto glory. Vision produces the strength of character to patiently endure the present discomfort and suffering for a better tomorrow. When you consider the glory ahead, you ignore the gloom of today. That is the power of vision.

VISION ENSURES THE PROMISE

The law of vision states that it is what you see that you receive. If you cannot see it, then forget it. "Then said the Lord unto men, thou has seen well: for I will hasten My Word to perform it" The Lord will not deny you what you have seen. Hallelujah! Many times, the Lord will not grant us the promise until He has ensured that we have seen it in our hearts.

VISION GIVES A MAN A SENSE OF RESPONSIBILITY

When you have a vision you are committed to, you become a responsible person. You cannot afford to live carelessly because your vision is your drive. The success or otherwise of your vision is your sole responsibility. Nobody can take the blame for your failure, you are accountable. This gives you a sense of responsibility and places your destiny in your own hands.

VISION PROMOTES DEVELOPMENT

Vision promotes a man. This is not just in terms of growth but more in terms of personal and overall development. Growth only means getting bigger, and it does not mean getting better. In fact, growth when it becomes uncontrolled becomes problematic giving rise to disease conditions like obesity and cancer. It also leads to chaos and disaster. Development on the other hand refers to a sustainable improvement in all areas of life. This is what vision does. It is vision that releases the potentials in you to become all you are created for.

VISION MAKES A MAN UNIQUE

The truth about you is that you are unique in your own way. Nobody is like you. Nobody can do the things you are capable of doing and nobody can replace you. Asserting this uniqueness lies in the power of your vision. The things you can envision and dream are unique to you and you alone. When you fulfil your visions, dreams and aspirations, you establish your relevance in life. In the absence of vision, you are just part of the whole lot of people going through life without purpose or sense of direction.

Chapter Six

The Singularity Of Vision

"The light of the body is in the eye: if therefore thine eye be single; the whole body shall be full of life". Mathew 6 v 2.

Possessing vision is of paramount importance in fulfilling purpose; however, it is not just enough to have a vision, it must be one with singularity of intention. This means clarity, simplicity, soundness and wholeness of vision. For your vision to produce the desired effect in your life, it must fulfil these criteria.

Clarity

"And the Lord answered me and said, write the vision and make it plain upon tables, that he may run that readeth it" Habakkuk 2 v 2.

The vision of what you want to be and have, must be clear in your mind and clearly stated on tables for it to have the power of achievement. What you are seeing and your destination needs no vagueness otherwise you will never arrive there. Until this settle, instability occasioned by conflicting interest will mar the effect of the vision. Clarity produces a state of definiteness and certainty. Also, it is not enough for your vision to be clear to you alone: it must also be easily understood by every person to whom you share it with. Once others are convinced of your vision, you will not lack resources both human and material to execute it.

Simplicity

Easy they say does it! A simple vision implies one that is easily achievable and easily communicable to others. A bogus and complicated vision breeds frustration. Some erroneously think that the more complex and sophisticated a vision is the more it will be appreciated. This is far from the truth! The advantage of making your vision simple is that it gives you a sense of accomplishment when it comes to fruition. Christianity itself is so simple, in all its ramifications that some people have felt they need to add some complexities to its practice. Make a vision simple for it to work.

Soundness

You vision needs to be sound to attract the attitude of sensible persons. It must be sound to the head, mind, soul and spirit. A sound vision receives the acceptance of all. Its appeal resides its soundness. No matter how out of the world your vision is, if it is sound, it will attract resources. Robert Schuller built an auditorium with a roof of glass having convinced his congregation of the soundness of his vision; he wanted to worship in an open heaven environment.

Wholeness

A vision should possess the attribute of being whole and complete. It is devoid of any defect whatsoever.

The vision should pass through scrutiny and survive it. A vision which lacks wholeness is that which lacks co-ordination and coherence. A complete vision brings every other thing in perfect unison towards the accomplishment of a common goal. It demands that you give yourself wholly (1 Timothy 4 v 5) to it. In addition, the fulfilment of the vision makes you a whole and complete person lacking in nothing whatsoever.

Chapter Seven

The Concept Of A Vision-Board

"YOU BECOME WHAT YOU BEHOLD"

"And the Lord answered me and said, write down the vision and make it plain upon tables, that he may run that readeth. For the vision is yet for an appointed time, but at the end it shall speak, and not a lie: though it tarry, wait for it: because it will surely come, it will not tarry" Habakkuk 2:2-3

The concept of a vision-board is enshrined in the scriptural passage quoted above. In the passage quoted above, the Lord told the prophet Habakkuk to write his vision down upon tables or a board to make it plain. He went to further state the power and efficacy of this vision-board by adding that whatever is written on it will surely come to pass and not fail. The only prerequisite was for the prophet to wait for the vision. This is what the concept of the vision-board is all about.

What Is A Vision-Board?

A vision-board is a powerful tool that enables you to visualize your dreams and visions. It keeps words and pictures that represent your vision in front of you each day so you never forget the reason behind the things you do. It is simply put a vision representation of the things you want to be, do or have in your life. It is also known as a goal map, treasure map. The whole idea of a vision-board is also encapsulated in the scripture that says "as a man thinketh in his heart, so is he" we tend to attract what we think; therefore if you surround yourself with the images of who you want to be, what you want to have etc. your life changes to conform to these images and our desires (2 Corinthians 3:18).

ELEMENTS OF A VISION-BOARD

A Vision-Board Must Be Visible

Jeremiah 1:11 says "what seeth thou" your vision-board must be visible as much as possible for you to have the power of performance. Your sub-conscious responds to images and pictures that impinge on your visual pathway. You ultimately become what you see. A visible vision-board ensures you are always seeing the right things you should be seeing. Otherwise you end up becoming what you did not want initially.

IT MUST BE EMOTIONAL

Your vision-board must contain pictures or images and words that elicit positive emotional responses from you. For it to have a positive impact on you, it must cause a release of adrenaline into your system. We are all emotional being and we respond to our emotions in such a profound way. Be it positive or negative emotions, we act in consonance with them. From the forgoing therefore, you need to surround yourself with pictures and images that evoke positive actions towards your goal.

IT MUST BE STRATEGICALLY LOCATED

To give you a maximum exposure on a daily basis, your vision-board must be strategically placed. It could be directly on your wardrobe, in your bedroom or as a screen saver on your laptop. Wherever place you choose, it must give you maximum exposure. Place it where you can always come across it many times in a day.

THE EFFECTS OF A VISION-BOARD

A vision-board that is visible enough to generate positive emotional response from you and that it is well placed for you to continually see undoubtedly produce effect on your life. Some of these effects are namely;

Creating a bridge between what is in your mind and what you can see and touch.

This is a powerful step towards taking action and making your vision a reality. It serves as a link or a connection between the realm of the unseen and the realm of the physical. The scripture says "calling those things that be not as though they were"

SERVING AS A CONSTANT REMINDER

Displaying your vision-board in a visible place serves as a constant reminder helping you to achieve those dreams and vision. One of the problems of vision is that without constant reminder, we tend to forget what the vision clearly states:

GIVING YOU THE POWER OF FOCUS

Vision-board produces focus with its unique power and attributes. It ensures you are not distracted from your primary goal and vision. As you look upon your vision-board on a daily basis, you are focused on how to realize same.

HOW TO CREATE A VISION-BOARD

Below are some practical steps on how to create a personal vision-board:

1. Locate scriptural verses and passages: there are scriptures that relate with the person you want to be, what you want to do and what you want to see in your life. Locate them. You can also

search through other resource materials like anointed books/magazines to locate pictures and inspirational words that fit into your dreams. Jesus said "search the scriptures for in them you think you have life, but they are they which testify of me" in another place, He said "lo I have come in the volume of books as it is written concerning Me; I have come to do Your will o Lord" He understood from the Word what His mission on earth was and He could not be distracted not by the wealth of the whole world nor the suffering in the hands of sinners.

2.   Prepare a cardboard paper: Get a beautiful cardboard that appeals to you. You can paint this cardboard to your desired taste that will appeal to you as you see them daily. Paint your future the way you want to see it right now and paste inspirational words from scripture on it. Get a picture of your dream house, your

dream car, your dream job etc. on this cardboard paper.

3.   Leave a space at the centre of the cardboard: Paste these words and picture on it. You could let it also contain your picture being surrounded by these words and images. This is a very good tool as it enables you to see yourself in your future. Wow! This is you in that tomorrow you have envisioned. Get a picture of yourself elegantly dressed and full of smile and excitement to represent your mood when the vision comes through.

4.   Lastly, hang your vision-board: On a very conspicuous place that you can see and relate with. Look at your vision-board every day and speak to yourself, declaring God's Word into your future.

Chapter Eight

Vision Stoppers

Certain attributes and character traits can make any vision no matter how promising lose its strength and effects for any man who wants and desires the fulfilment of his vision, these vision stoppers must be avoided and stopped by all means before they stop you.

Laziness

"The sluggard will not plow by reason of the cold; therefore shall he beg in

harvest, and have nothing" Proverbs 20 v 4

To be lazy means unwillingness to do any work or to make an effort. It is the bane of any vision. If you are unwilling to make any effort about your vision, you can never come to fulfilment. You could make the loudest noise but you will never be able to accomplish those dreams and aspirations. You are a loser from the onset and there is no amount of prayer or fasting that could suffice it.

FOUR FACTS ABOUT THE LAZY MAN

(i)   He is a wishful-thinker: The lazy man desires the best of things but ends up getting nothing. The reason is not far-fetched; he will not put his hands to work. The scriptures states that he that will not work should not eat. Indeed if wishes were horses, beggars would ride on one!

(ii)   He is an excuse maker: There are always a thousand and one reasons why the job cannot be done for the lazy man. He makes the most senseless excuses for his laziness. He says there is a lion in the way: a lion is in the street. In-fact some excuses may be real, but the lazy man exaggerates them and commits nothing to overcome the limitations

(iii)   He lacks business activity: He does not possess any business acumen and when put in charge of any business he ruins it because he is slothful, lazy and careless. No business thrives in the hand of a lazy man. Others wake up early to go about their business; he on the other hand sees no sense in the stress.

(iv)   He is a great waster: A lazy man neglects his work and allows every good thing to waste. He is a brother to him who actually destroys his work.

Ignorance

"For by wise counsel thou shalt make thy war: and in the multitude of counsellors there is safety" – Proverbs 24 v 6.

One of the great stoppers of vision is ignorance. Lack of knowledge and insight will make the best vision redundant and eventually perish. In the first place, ignorance will preclude a man from having a vision and if he does have one, that vision will never come to light. As a matter of fact, the level of your knowledge will determine the quality of your vision. A learned man will obviously have a brighter vision because his knowledge comes to play in what he can see and imagine. A vision based on facts of knowledge either of God's Word or on necessary information becomes solid. Furthermore, knowledge will increase your strength and speed in the fulfilment of your vision. The time spent in acquiring information concerning an area of interest is far more compensated for in the speed of accomplishment in the long run. The role of counsellors in vision fulfilment cannot be overemphasized! By wise counsel, the scripture says you shall make thy war. Also by wise counsel, vision is sustained, by wise counsel, vision is actualized. By all means seek counsel and your vision will be realized.

Wrong Company

"If any man obeys not our word, have no company with him" 2 Thessalonians 3 v 14.

It has been established earlier that you need people to achieve your vision and dreams, however beware of bad company. You do not need everybody on your way to fulfilling destiny. In the real sense of it. Some people are positioned to cancel your dreams. This they do by way of wrong counsel, lack of faith in our dreams and sarcastic comments passed on the vision.

For instance, David had three major discouragements on his way to defeating goliath. One of the most formidable obstacles was from his own brother Eliab. He was reprimanded for daring to think of engaging goliath in battle. His response? "he turned from him towards another" If David had followed his brother's sarcastic comment, goliath would have not only defeated Israel but also David's testimony would have been cut short by one. Dissociate yourself from anyone who belittles your vision no matter the bond that keeps you together! Some people will never see your vision the way you see it no matter how hard you explain it. Instead of seeing the good in you and your dreams, these dream haters only see the negative aspect and will not stop until they stop you and your vision beware of them!

Inordinate Affection

"How then can I do this great wickedness and sin against God" Genesis 39 v 9.

Inordinate affection refers to an excessive show of affection beyond reasonable limit of degree. It also means showing lack of restraint or control in the display of affection. Not a few vision and dreams have been aborted and truncated by inordinate affection. It cuts short every tall dream and aspiration whenever it rears its ugly head. Joseph would have definitely lost his place in destiny and ultimately in the plans and purpose of God if he had succumbed to Mrs Potiphar's wish.

Samson with all the great promises of being Israel's mighty deliverer ended up dying with the enemy because of lack of control over his affections. As a young person, one of the great vision stoppers to deal with is inordinate affection. Self-control and self-discipline should be your watch if you must fulfil your dreams.

Have control over your appetite, your desires and draw the line in your relationships if you want to see that dream come to pass. You have been given the grace to say no to all ungodliness. That is self-control and self-discipline.

Fear

"Why are ye so fearful? How is it that ye have no faith"?

Fear is the number one thief of vision. It stops you from doing what you could have done. It deprives you of the joy of accomplishment by preventing you from starting at all. Fear of failure has prevented the birth of great visions, has deprived many of achieving success and has kept not a few visions imprisoned. As a result of fear of the giants and the children of the Anak, the ten spies sent along-side Caleb and Joshua gave an evil report to the children of Israel. How the children of Israel wept sore! They were ready to forgo the Promised Land because of fear. Their dream of entering Canaan was on the verge of being thwarted but for the courage and faith of Joshua and Caleb. Not only does fear prevent, it also torments the owner. The Bible says "say to them that are of a fearful heart, be strong and fear not" (Isaiah 35 v 4). I say to you all who have allowed fear to cage your vision be strong and fear not, your God will come and help you.

Anywhere fear is found, faith is absent. The two cannot co-habit, they are mutually exclusive. Faith in God and your God-given ability is a necessary tool in the accomplishment of vision. When fear steps in the pursuit of your vision, remember God has not given you the spirit of fear but of love, of power and of a sound mind.

Negative Effects Of Fear

1.   Fear stops you from doing anything worthwhile. Fear is a stopper

2.   It predisposes to errors. The fearful person messes things up because he is nervous, anxious and apprehensive.

3.   It drains your energy. The sympathetic discharges generated in fear are wasted in doing nothing in particular.

Pride

"Pride goeth before destruction and a haughty spirit before a fall" Proverbs 16 v 18

Pride is a recognized destroyer of vision. History books are filled with the dangers of pride as empires, kingdoms and business estates have all fallen due to the ill effects of pride. Any man with a vision and who desires his dream to come to pass must avoid pride like a plaque otherwise his tall vision will become a piece of rubbish fit only for the trash bin

Reasons Why Pride Negates Any Vision

God resists the proud: James 4 v 6

When pride was found in Lucifer, God brought him down from his exalted position. Why King Nebuchadnezzar became exalted in pride, he had his abode with the wild animals for seven seasons. King Herod was devoured alive by worms the day he accommodated pride in his heart. A man who is proud makes himself an enemy of the Almighty.

Pride is a turn-off:

A proud man turns off anyone he comes in contact with. When he needs help, he will not acknowledge it and he will not find anybody's ready for assistance. He does not seek counsel from others neither does he accept advice from elders. A man of vision cannot afford to be wise in his own eyes because he needs people to accomplish his vision.

Disobedience

"If ye be willing and obedient, ye shall eat the good of the land" – Isaiah 1 v 18.

Every vision succumbs to ills of disobedience. To disobey instructions from someone higher and more knowledgeable than you will lead to abortion of your vision.

Many have walked the path of disobedience and have had only themselves to blame for their woes in life, often times the effort directed at correcting the mistakes caused by disobedience amounts to an unnecessary waste of resources and time. Every time the children of Israel disobeyed God, they paid for it dearly: some lost/lose their lives while others had to wait longer than planned to get to Canaan. Samson disobeyed his parents and married Delilah and paid for it with his life and the abortion of his ministry and destiny. No man ever escaped the consequences of disobedience no matter how little or big.

The Bible says that "If ye be willing and obedient" Obedience is the key that unlocks the treasures of heaven. It is that attribute that attracts favour and blessing. Abraham was declared blessed because he choose to obey God though it was hard. His obedience brought unprecedented blessings upon him and generations after him. If you desire to fulfil destiny and see your dreams come to pass, learn to be obedient in all spheres of life. You must obey even in the midst of pain and stress. Choose obedience above disobedience, choose to seek instructions and follow them and you will arrive in your desired heaven. The question that readily beg for answers is this: who should I obey?

God: He is the master instructor and our God. He guides us on the path to take for our sakes. When He corrects us, it is for our good.

Parents: Your parents are your God-given guardians on earth. The Bible enjoins us to obey our parents and it is the first commandment with a blessing no matter who you are, you cannot grow above your parents.

Mentor: They represent our life-coach. In a football team, the role of a coach cannot be downplayed the best of players require the guidance of a coach to reach their peak performance. Likewise you need to obey your mentors as you aspire to reach your goal.

Chapter Nine

Overcoming Vision Stoppers

Lessons from the Life of Joseph

In this chapter, we shall be considering the life of Joseph in a little more detailed form to learn how he was able to overcome the series of vision stoppers that came his way.

His Birth

Joseph was the first child of Rachael Jacob's beloved wife. His father had laboured for fourteen years to gain Racheal's hand in marriage instead of the initial agreed seven years. After their marriage, Racheal could not give Jacob a child for many years. How this couple waited and longed for the first fruit of their love. It was waiting period of frustration nobody would dwindle for.

On the other hand, Leah – Racheal's elder sister and rival at home was providing Jacob with sons. The more Jacob and Racheal prayed for a child, the more God was opening the womb of Leah. However no matter the number of children Leah was producing, Jacob's desire and prayer for his wife Racheal never ceased. It was a longing that nothing else (not even six sons and daughters) could fill. On the side of Racheal, it was like "what is wrong with love" what a situation.

It was under this condition that Racheal discovered that she was pregnant. She obviously could not keep the news to herself as she rushed to announce it to her beloved husband Jacob. Right from that first day, the case of Joseph (yet unborn) began. Racheal did not lack anything during her antenatal periods. She had the best of care during this period because nothing must go wrong with this baby. Jacob began to save very big for his unborn prince. When Joseph was eventually born, he had a very "big" silver spoon in his mouth.

His Childhood

"And Israel loved Joseph more than all his sons because Joseph was born when he was an old man" Genesis 37 v 3.

Evidently Joseph had the best of childhood. He was lavished with love and affection beyond measure. He was given the best training money could afford. To express his feelings for his sons, Jacob made him a coat of many colours. He became the envy of his siblings and he cared less about it. He enjoyed every attention his parents paid to him and no child could have asked for more!

His Dreams:

"He said to them, listen to the dream that I have had" Genesis 37 v 6.

Joseph was a great dreamer and he could not but tell his dreams to his world – his brothers and parents. He was so convinced of the authenticity of his dreams that he began to live as such. In his first dream, he saw the bundle of grains he had gathered rise up among the others and his brothers bundles were bowing down to it. It means a lot to him that he wasted no time to announce it to them. When his brothers heard this dream, they were very angry as the meaning was clear to them. Joseph was going to be a ruler over them! How they fumed and cursed but the young man was not disillusioned at all.

He yet had another dream; the sun and moon and the eleven stars were bowing to him. This was the last stroke that broke the camel's back. This time even Jacob could not help but exclaimed "what is this dream that you have had, Joseph could not stop talking of his dreams even if it meant incurring the wrath of both friends and foes he just kept saying it until it became so real to him.

His Journey

The fulfilment of Joseph's dream would be in the palace of Egypt. However tortuous was the route from the comfort and luxury of his father's house to the palace – his place of fulfilment. It was no easy road and many were the vision stoppers that contend with him. His antidote against these stoppers forms our object of discussion.

Joseph Was Faithful And Hardworking:

Right from his days at his father's house to his tenure as Egypt's prime minister, Joseph distinguished himself in service and in integrity. He was not lazy at all and was not found wanting in all he had to do. In-fact, in Potiphar's house, he had an excellent testimony. He was so hardworking and had the evidence of God's approval that his master made him ruler over his household. Everything he laid his hand upon prospered. When he got to the prison, the chief warder saw these attributes and promptly crowned him the chief in prison. Indeed, the diligent hand beareth rule. Proverbs 12 v 24).

He Was Knowledgeable:

Having been given the best education as a child, Joseph grew in knowledge. He learnt the customs of his fathers and quickly adapted to the culture of Egypt. He understood writings and traditions. Everywhere he served en route the palace, he left no one in doubt about his wisdom after interpreting pharaoh's dreams, the king was amazed at his wisdom and quickly appointed him his prime minister. Joseph definitely was not an ignorant man: he was a man of knowledge.

He Resisted Temptation

While attending to his daily chores one fateful morning, madam Potiphar came behind and grabbed his coat. Lie with me she said. She had made several advances to Joseph which on each occasion he had refused. On this occasion, he not only resisted but ran for his destiny "how can I do this great wickedness and sin against God" were his last word before he thinks of leaving his garment behind with the madam. The Bible says "flee from all appearances of evil" that is the way every man with a dream handles temptation. If Joseph had co-operated with madam that day, he would have negotiated his dream and ended up at best the most handsomely paid servant in Egypt perhaps, with an official residence and a car assigned to him courtesy of Mrs Potiphar.

He Was Fearless And Courageous

Joseph was fearless and very courageous. He did not mind what his brothers could do to him. Even when in Egypt, his anchor was in God. The psalmist says "I put my trust in God; I shall not fear what man can do to me" that was one of Joseph's favourite scriptures I presume. He did not permit fear to stop him from announcing his vision the second time despite the anger and envy the first one generated. He was courageous enough to run from madam even though he was a bloody servant in the house. He spoke the truth even when the truth meant death sentence to the baker. This characterized his life throughout and he eventually fulfilled his dreams.

He Was Humble In Prosperity

His humility despite his privileged background was infectious. Very few would keep their heads low if they had the kind of background Joseph had. When he came into position as second – in – command in Egypt; a position no other foreigner in Egypt ever occupied, he kept his cool. He became so wealthy and wielded so much power yet he was humble in his dealings. At a time when he could have revenged the unfair and negative treatment his brothers melted out to him, he was shedding tears of affection. His humility made God to be committed to him; it attracted many to him and made him to last long on the throne as prime minister. The Holy Scriptures rightly says that "Humble thyself under the mighty hands of God and in due time He will exalt you".

He Was An Obedient Man

Joseph was obedient to a fault. When his father Jacob sent him to the field to find out how his brothers were doing, he promptly obeyed. He obeyed his father even though he knew it was a risky venture. He was going to meet people who resented him greatly partly because of their father's obvious favouritism and partly because of his dreams. He was an obedient servant in Potiphar's house and in the prison; he complied with every prison regulations that he soon became a captain in prison. He never rebelled against constituted authority and neither had any query issued against him for insubordination he simply obeyed all!

Joseph no doubt fulfilled his childhood dreams. He became all God had planned for him. He became the leader and ruler his brothers were wrath with him over. He survived and overcame all the vision stoppers the devil planted in his way. His story is an encouragement to any dreamer and anyone who would dare to have a vision for life. All you need to do in order to overcome and triumph over vision stoppers is to follow Joseph's steps. You cannot miss it.

Chapter Ten

Preserving the Vision

Not everybody who failed in life started out without a vision. In-fact many people dream big and desire big things but many of these dreams are lost somewhere along the line. A lot of visions have either been corrupted or negotiated short of their original state. Many who started well lost steam and failed to end well. Worse still, quite a number end up with a corrupted version of their vision. They have what looks like the vision but somehow and somewhere, the enemy has succeeded in cheating on their vision. It is therefore very imperative that after possessing a vision and overcoming stoppers of vision, all efforts must be put in place to preserve the vision. Remember if the devil cannot stop your vision, he will leave no stone unturned to try to corrupt it. What then you have at the end of the day is remotely different from the original vision if he succeeds.

Definition

Preserving your vision means

Keeping the quality and features of your vision

Every vision has its core qualities that are unique in all ramifications. These qualities make the vision what it is and what it represents. They are the essence, the real thing in the vision. Remove or corrupt these qualities then you have a completely different thing entirely.

As a visionary, it is your sole responsibility to keep these unique features of your vision intact. A lot of people permit others to add or even remove certain elements to or from their vision in the guise of counselling. By the time the counselling session is over, you will suddenly discover that though it was counselling you went for, you end up having your vision cancelled. If we carry out the statistics of some visions especially in terms of denominations, we will find out that many of the denominations in the body of Christ today did not actually start out as such. Many began like fellowship centres and Bible study groups and were paraded as such only, for the core values these centres represented to be changed. What started out as an evening meeting began to snowball into Sunday worship and so on. The leader who was known as brother so and so soon began to bear titles like founder and bishop. God help us!

Keeping Your Vision In Its Original State And In Good Condition

"And the angels which kept not their first estate, but left their own habitation, He hath reserved in everlasting chains under darkness unto judgment of the great day" – Jude 1 v 6.

It is not just enough to have a vision in the beginning: it becomes more important to strive to keep that vision intact in its original state. It is a duty that every man or woman who has a vision must endeavour to do. Also, to keep the vision in its original state is but one step of the job; the most relevant is that, the vision must be kept in good condition.

To claim to have a vision twenty years ago and you can still clearly remember it word for word without any significant work done on it amount to disaster. Yes, you have kept the vision in its original, undiluted state; however you have failed to keep it in good condition. You are like the wicked servant who dug the ground to keep the money his master gave him to trade with and made no profit whatsoever.

Consequences Of Not Preserving The Vision

It Breeds Confusion

A man who has had his vision changed from its original state will live a very confused life. He started out with something but now doing another thing completely. He keeps getting tossed here and there not knowing what exactly to pursue. He is the "anything goes man" today he hears this is what is in vogue and he runs after it and tomorrow he hears something else and abandons the former to follow the new. He is inconsistent and cannot be trusted with anything worthwhile.

The Bible says *"that we henceforth be no more children tossed to and fro and carried about with every wind of doctrine, by the sleight of men and cunning craftiness, whereby they live in wait to deceive"* (Ephesians 4 v 14).

The confused man is likened to a child who is tossed to and fro and carried about with the rave of the moment he has no real standing and as such cannot achieve anything good.

It Amounts To Doing Someone Else's Work

Once your vision becomes corrupted, you begin to follow and do another person's assignment. You have derailed from your own task and began to carry another man's responsibility some people specializes in turning other people's vision to suit theirs.

Such people use others to achieve their selfish goals.

Vision Preservatives

Vision preservatives refer to those qualities that every visionary must possess in order to preserve his/her God-given vision. These are the things that are needed to prevent your vision from going sour and corrupted.

These are:

1. Daily confession:

"This book is of the law shall not depart from your mouth but in it thou shall meditate day and night and thou shall make thy way prosperous and thou shall have good success" – Joshua 1 v 8

The number one vision preservative is daily confession of your vision. You need to confess who you are in Christ Jesus and what you are created to be on a daily basis. To preserve the quality and integrity of your vision, it becomes a necessity for you to declare it first to yourself and then to others who care to listen.

Your vision must not depart from your mouth if you want to be prosperous in it. Keep saying it even when it does not look like it.

Daily confession will help you in a number of ways namely:

It produces faith in your heart: the scripture 2 Corinthians 4 v13 says, ***"having the same spirit of faith; we believe and therefore we speak"*** the more you say what you want to be and have, the more faith grows in your heart.

You will prosper in the vision: one route to prosperity is the mouth, God told Joshua that if you desire to prosper, the book of the law must not depart from your mouth. It is very true when it comes to vision too.

Lastly, you will preserve your vision in its original state: permit me to say this; your mouth is your preservative. Use it well.

1.   Complete Understanding

In an earlier chapter, we established that one of the ways to achieve your vision is to know your vision inside-out. It is no less a preservative of a vision. There is no amount of manipulation and scheming that will corrupt what you have once you have a perfect understanding of it.

Whether they turn it to the right or left, you are in control because you have a complete insight into it. An example of how a complete understanding of a vision helps to preserve the vision can be seen in the life of Moses in the place of Egypt. King Pharaoh negotiated with him on several occasions on the deliverance of the children of Israel. He was not deceived because he knew too well what instructions he received from the Lord. In verse 26 of exodus chapter 10, Moses said to Pharaoh *"our cattle also shall go with us, there shall a hoof be left behind; for thereof must we take to serve the Lord our God: and we know not with what we must serve the Lord, until we come thither"* this is a perfect understanding of vision and assignment.

Moses could have contended himself with leaving the animals behind since the promise of deliverance was to the people. However, he knew that it was not just liberation but liberty to serve God. To serve God well requires those animals that Pharaoh wanted to be left behind. What an insight!

The devil still uses that trick these days. He tells you all sort of lies like you don't require money/materials to be a good Christian. Wait a minute with what will you serve the Lord with if you leave the wealth behind to the world.

2.   Go The Extra Mile

Many of God's children today are carrying about a disjointed and corrupted vision because of inability to go the extra mile, to do the extra thing. Some are happy with little they have now simply because they are not prepared to pay the prize for the ultimate. There is an ultimate in every vision and it takes the man who is ready to go the extra mile to do the extra to achieve it.

Jacob wanted Rachael and was told the bride prize was seven years of servitude in Laban's house. After he paid the agreed prize, he was denied of his dream based on tradition and custom. Instead of his ultimate, he was offered Leah to Rachael. It will require another seven years of labour. Jacob was determined to preserve the vision of taking Rachael as wife and he served the required years and at the end she became his wife. How many years all together did Jacob labour for Rachael? 14 years.

For many, Leah was good enough at the sight of another seven years. A woman is a woman whether her name is Leah or Racheal. Why bother with extra number of years when at least I have a wife already? Does that sound familiar? It is the voice we hear on a daily basis trying to persuade us to forgo our initial and original plan. You wanted to acquire a university degree from the onset but because you have not been able to pass the entrance examination, another certificate becomes gratifying. It is inability to go the extra mile. Inability to persevere a little longer often denies one from getting the ultimate in life.

3. Stay Focused

The power of focus in the preservation of a vision is not in doubt, your vision cannot be corrupted as long as you stay focused on it. Focus according to the Encarta dictionary is defined as "concentrated efforts or attention on a particular thing" when you concentrate on your vision, you will guard it like a mother hen would guard her young. Every attempt by the devil or anyone to suggest anything outside the "core" of your vision will be fully resisted because your attention is on it.

If you must keep intact the integrity of your vision, you must stay focused on it. That is the only thing that is needful in visions. Many have allowed the applause of others tilt them to completely different missions in life. Others have allowed the enemy's wiles to deceive them out of their initial goals and set objective. Remember, you owe no man any explanation whatsoever, except the God who gave you the vision initially.

4.   Avoid Covetousness:

"And saith unto him, all these things will I give thee if thou wilt fall down and worship me" Mathew 4 v 9.

The vision and mission of Jesus to planet earth was clear from the beginning. The angel that visited Mary told her about his vision and in-fact the name Jesus means that He will deliver His people from their sins. Nevertheless, at the start of that mission, the enemy came to negotiate this very mission. He took Jesus to an exceedingly high mountain and showed him all the kingdoms of the world from

Asia to Europe to all six continents of the world. He also displayed the glories of thesekingdoms before Him, all these will be yours if You can forgo what You came here for; was the devils offer.

The devil still uses the same old tactics to dissuade people from their vision. It is the book of covetousness. He offers "quicker" and "shorter" route to the end and leads the unwise away from the original designed path. Multitudes have fallen prey to this and only live there after to lick their wounds. Many dreams and aspirations have been sacrificed on the altar of covetousness. Very many promising visions have been substituted on this road and you must avoid this menace with all you have got to reach your desired goal.

Jesus responded thus "get thee hence, satan: for it is written" a powerful reply to the spirit of covetousness, no consideration and no negotiation at all. This was how eve missed it in the Garden of Eden. The Bible says she looked at the fruit and saw that it was good for eating. No matter how tempting the offer is, if it will corrupt your vision, throw it away. Don't even consider and think twice about it. Note this; what the enemy is offering you now is already yours: it is a matter of time you will get there. So don't permit him to substitute your vision because of a "pot of porridge".

5.   Warfare Prayers

"Fight the good fight of faith, lay hold on eternal life, whereunto thou art also called and hast professed good profession before many witnesses" 1 Timothy 6 v 12

Vision accomplishment is warfare believe it or not. It is serious business and it requires that you give your all as you strive towards its fulfilment. The only fight you are permitted to engage in is the fight for your vision. A fight for your vision is actually a fight for your life. If you chicken out now, you are probably worse than the person who did not possess a vision at first.

There are seen and unseen forces militating against your vision. They come in many subtly ways; they are indeed enemies of your vision. Rise up to defend your vision from corruption and from substitution. Do not wake in the middle of the night to discover it is a "dead child" that is lying with.alas your "real living child" has been stolen.

Chapter Eleven

Re-Inventing Your Vision

"For a just man falleth seven times and rises up again" Proverbs 24 v 16.

Several people have witnessed disappointments, corruption and some outright cancellation of their visions. Not a few individuals though alive, yet their vision have long ceased to exist. For these ones, life has lost its flavour and has become an endurance trek. Others cannot move forward nor can they turn backwards. They have become trapped and stranded in life. To such people, there is yet another opportunity to re-invent their visions.

A vision goes through many life-cycles during a man's life time. You may be in the phase of disquietedness and there seems to be no light in the horizon. Don't worry or despair, it's time to re-launch, it's time to re-invent and re-invigorate your vision.

May be you have fallen seven times already; God is the God of another chance. You are not finished yet; there is more in you waiting to be re-launched it is time for vision re-loaded.

There is a story of a Nigerian footballer that has really encouraged many all over the world. His name is KanuNwankwo. After the 1996 Atlanta Olympics where he led the Nigerian football team to gold in the men's football event, he was diagnosed with heart disease. It came to many as a rude shock. However, this hero of Nigerian football rose from this seemingly difficult set back and re-launched himself into the football world.

Another story worthy of note is that Zambian national team. The whole team perished in a plane crash on their way to honour an international match in 1993. It was a national disaster, nobody expected that country to be relevant in African football for the next decade alas they came back stronger in 1994 at Africa nation's cup hosted in Tunisia. They came second behind Nigeria. What the team did was to simply re-invent their vision and they really show cased the resilience of vision.

There are two people in the scripture that showed us the way forward after a seemingly lost or corrupted vision. We shall be looking at their lives with hope that we could gain insight of our own.

Vision re-invent or vision re-launch is possible for the never say die person.

Samson

Samson was a child of prophesy born to be a deliverer and a judge in Israel. His parents having being visited by an angel from God where given specific instructions on his upbringing. His birth was with so much hope and enthusiasm a hope of a whole nation. He must not fail to deliver or else the whole country would be in continual bondage.

He started out well killing and tormenting the enemy. The fear of Samson went around the enemy's camp. His fame went far and wild; many exploits were done by him. He has a full understanding of his vision and was living it. The philistines were in trouble as long as Samson kept the vision, he was unstoppable! Alas, there was a shift in his focus. Samson had a major distraction, his involvement with a philistine woman cost him his vision. The secret to his anointing was known which rendered him incapacitated. The enemy dealt with him, the deliverer became a bond man.

The hope of Israel was bound hand and foot; his eyes plucked out and vision corrupted. But in the midst of all these, he began to pray to God for his vision/mission to be re-invented. The purpose for which he was born and his mission to secure the nation of Israel. The scripture says "and his hair began to grow again" judges 16 v 22. With his vision re-invented and re-loaded, he killed more people at the end than he did earlier on. Permit me to quickly add this: the achievement of a man with a re-loaded vision far outweigh the initial achievement. There is certainly hope for you no matter what blow has been dealt to your vision.

The Prodigal Son

A father woke up one morning to be met by his younger son demanding for his birth right "give me the portion that falleth to me" was his audacious request. He had a vision to go into a far country and get a living for himself. His request was granted and off he went with the substance needed to pursue a life vision.

However in the far country, he met with some persons who corrupted and destroyed his original vision. Within a twinkle of an eye, this young man wasted all his substance in riotous living. What he set out to accomplish initially was lost and he focused on other visionary activities. The Result was that he became a beggar desiring to feed with a herd of swine. What a fall from grace to grass.

One day the Bible says he came back to his senses and said "I will arise and go to my father to be restored" and immediately he arose and set out for his homeward journey back to his father; to the source of his original vision. Gladly too, his father has been waiting for such a time when he would return. The prodigal son was not only re-admitted by his father, he had his place restored to him. Maybe you have been prodigious with your vision and now you cannot really say for sure what direction your life is going. There is plenty of room for you in the father's heart. Your vision is waiting to be re-invented. Just be bold to take that journey back home no matter how far you have strayed.

How To Re-Invent Your Vision

There are practical steps to take in order to re-invent your vision. They are in themselves not exhaustive but they are guidelines you can follow:

1. Locate where you have missed it: This is the first step towards vision re-invent. You need to be able to locate the exact area where things have gone wrong. What wrong step did you take or what wrong association did you enter into that corrupted your vision? This is important as you need to make a U-turn, repent and return to the first things you started with. Samson entered into a relationship with Delilah and it cost him his eyes- his vision. He expired long before his time. The prodigal son left home earlier than his time and had bad company that corrupted his vision.

Thanks be to God that these two men realized they had missed and found their way back. Samson on the other hand killed more philistines at his death than previously and the prodigal son got his position restored in his father's house. It all starts from locating where you missed it.

2. Locate courage to start again: Many who desire to pick up the pieces of their lives often find it difficult to start again. Some think they cannot face the shame of admitting failure, others feel their friends and colleagues have left them behind and to start from the scratch is unthinkable. If you are serious about re-inventing your vision, no amount of discouragement will be strong enough to hinder you. Be strong and courageous, start again; just do it again.

Locating where you have missed it and your core values are not enough to re-invent your vision. These only will produce outright self-pity and frustration. However taking a bold step and starting where you stopped is the key. Let your passion drive you again, let your core values be your energizer. You cannot allow it to end here, pick up the wretch and make it work again.

Chapter Twelve

By Vision You Can kick-Start a Brighter Future

"Am about to die; of what use is birth right to me"? Genesis 25 v 32

Vision has given birth to great inventions of our time, has provided answers to human needs and aspirations and above all has changed the course of humanity. Vision is the tool the creator has given to man to influence his world. That you need a vision if you dream of imparting your world positively is in no doubt. It is vision that will enable you to take advantage of everything around you be it good or bad. Adversity to a man of vision is simply an advantage locked behind bars: a setback is a spring board for higher achievement and failure is a fortune waiting to be explored. To him who has a vision, this scripture is very true "all things work together for good" (Romans 8 v 28). He sees opportunity for greatness whenever things do not go according to plans. He is very versatile and adapts to everything around him to work for him. Nothing indeed can stop a man with vision.

However, to be bereaved of vision is the beginning of every failure in life. Opportunities slip away without recognition and greatness is wasted on the altar of carelessness. Esau was an epitome of a man without vision. He saw no good in his birth right and was quick to dispose of it for a plate of his brother's porridge.

He lost both the birth right and his place in destiny. When the time for the blessing of the first born came, it was then he realized that he was no longer qualified he had substituted his blessing with food!

On the other hand, Jacob a man of vision and great insight saw the significance of birth right and used what he had for what he felt he needed. I can imagine when Isaac was pronouncing the blessing on him; he must have felt fulfilled having paid for it in full with his food. That distinguishes a man of vision. He knows he does not possess everything he requires to reach his goal but he is prepared to use what he has got to gain what he does not have.

When you bow your knees in prayer, above all, ask God to give you a vision for your life. You will never be the same again. You cannot afford to live a life devoid of vision as from today onwards.

With all you have seek vision both for your life and what God has designed you to be. Live each day with the mind-set that you are getting closer to your destiny. At the end of each day, do a personal audit on your performance and how well you have lived out your vision. Yes you can live out your dreams; you can climb to the top of your career and you can be the best ever.

Through vision, many have over taken their older ones just like Jacob. The younger has rule over his entire household and even saved them from starvation. Life does not necessary answer to "first come, first serve" principle. Jesus once said that some who come first will be last. It is all about vision. Age is not a relevant factor in the matters of life and destiny. A king had ruled at age eight in Israel and young people have dominated business and world politics even Christian ministry. It is high time a man judged not by his age or background but by the content of his vision. I have seen people who became the first in their families to become university graduates. Some others have broken the jinx of many generations by being the first to have successful marriages and build houses. Do not let what has been to deter you from being what you could be. Yesterday only possesses the power you give to it and your tomorrow is a product of your vision today. Nobody knows you enough to determine what you can achieve and what you can have in life. You are the only limiting factor to your destiny!

The authority (power) of vision is all about being bold enough to look at yourself in the mirror of God's Word and to come to terms with who it says you are. It is about dreaming bigger than your limitations and achieving greatness even though your background has nothing to write home about.

The courage to announce your vision and follow it through no matter the obstacles along your way is required in authority(power) of vision.

You can break that circle of poverty that has run in your lineage for years. You can become the beginning of another lineage with positive accolades. The generations yet unborn are calling on you to help kick-start a brighter future they can be proud of. You can do it and you must not fail. It is all in the possibility of vision.

Seth the third in line from Adam started a generation of people who began to call on the name of the Lord. Noah had the privilege of being the patriarch of the "post-flood world" by simply following instructions he received from God. Abraham became the father of faith having obtained a good report that he pleased God. Nelson Mandela, Tambo Mbeki and a host of others are founding fathers of the nation South Africa, because they had the vision of an independent country. The list is without end of people who despite the prevailing situations of their world, rose above them and created the path of freedom and prosperity other generations later would follow.

Somebody started the good we celebrate today. South Africa cannot be complete without the story and vision of Nelson Mandela for a free nation where black and white people can leave freely. Your Future is You!